THIS BOOK IS PRESENTED TO:

-- -- -- -- -- -- -- -- -- -- -- -- -- -- -- --

ON THE OCCASION OF:

-- -- -- -- -- -- -- -- -- -- -- -- -- -- -- --

AS A SPECIAL GIFT/ ~~████~~

PROVOCATIVE GESTURE* FROM:

-- -- -- -- -- -- -- -- -- -- -- -- -- -- -- --

BECAUSE:

-- -- -- -- -- -- -- -- -- -- -- -- -- -- --

-- -- -- -- -- -- -- -- -- -- -- -- -- -- -- --

AND:

-- -- -- -- -- -- -- -- -- -- -- -- -- -- -- --

-- -- -- -- -- -- -- -- -- -- -- -- -- -- -- --

* DELETE AS APPROPRIATE

PREPARE
YOURSELF

HOW I FLY;

TRAY TABLE DOWN

LAPTOP P.C.

MOBILE PHONE

WALKMAN

FAG

SEAT BACK

6

DRAWINGS I DO;

FUCK

THE BOOK OF

SHRIGLEY

REDSTONE

Edited by Mel Gooding and Julian Rothenstein

First published in 2005 by

Redstone Press

7a St Lawrence Terrace, London W10 5SU

Tel 020 7352 1594 Fax 020 7352 8749

email jr@redstonepress.co.uk

website www.redstonepress.co.uk

ISBN 1 870003 24 1

Book design: Julian Rothenstein

Artwork: Terence Smiyan, Jessica Taylor

Production: Tim Chester

Printed and bound by C&C Offset Printing Co.,Ltd , China

Thanks to

Gaby Agis, Hilary Arnold, David Bellingham, Bookworks, BQ Cologne, Miranda Davies, Pete Donaldson, Brian Durrans,

Charles Esche, Alec Finlay, Stephen Friedman Gallery, Frieze, Rhiannon Gooding, Rupert Harris, Yoris Van De Horst,

Cameron Jamie, Hiang Kee, Anton Kern Gallery, Galerie Yvon Lambert, Kim McKinney (especially), Nieves, Galerie

Francesca Pia, Stan Shepherd, Transmission Gallery, Toby Webster, Galleri Nicolai Wallner.

THIS BOOK BELONGS TO:
DAVID SHRIGLEY, 1/L, 23, BENTINCK ST., GLASGOW ~~xxxx~~
TEL ~~xxxxxxxxxx~~

| START | 20/4/95 | FIN | 8·8·95 |

IT'S FREEZING IN HERE

with my careful shouts and doggerel poems I hope to alter the ways of the bad people

USE OF RED INK WITH BLACK INK TO HIGHLIGHT MISTAKES

GRAFFITI's
GRAFITTI

at~~te~~pmt
ATTEMPT

APPENDIX ✓

KEY ✓

FORIEGN
FOREIGN

POCess
POSSESS   POSESSIONS

LEGEND "LE GENT"

watermark

MAPS

CONTENTS ✓

sub-head

LIST OF ILLUSTRATIONS ✓

FOOTNOTES ✓   DRAWINGS

SPECIMEN PAGE ✓

THE INTRODUCTION ✓

EDITORS NOTE

PRINTED HALF-OFF THE PAGE

CONCLUSION

PREFACE ✓

BASTARD TITLE

HALF TITLE

AUTHOR'S NOTE ✓

PUBLISHER'S NOTE ✓

TRANSLATOR'S NOTE

FRONTISPIECE

BACK TO FRONT

LIST OF MAPS

DUST JACKET ✓

FURTHER READIN' ✓

trying to think of new things to say

FOREWORD ✓

ACKNOWLEDGEMENTS ✓

ALTERNATIVE ENDINGS ✓

GLOSSARY ✓

EPILOGUE

FOOTNOTES ✓   BIBLIOGRAPHY

INDEX ✓

NOTES ✓

FURTHER READING:

LIFE , OR, IS THAT IT ?

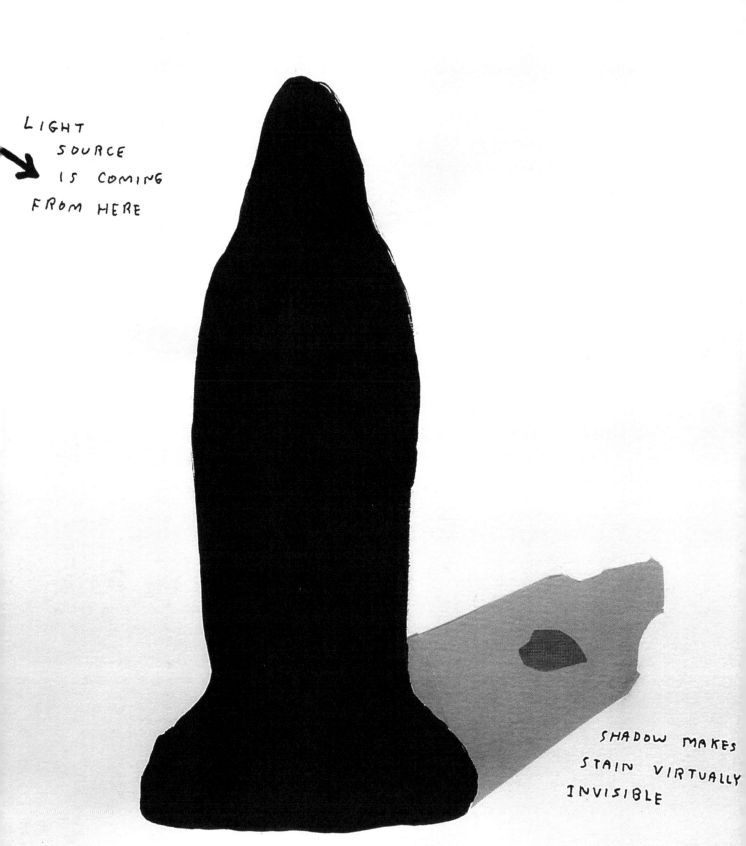

LIGHT SOURCE IS COMING FROM HERE

SHADOW MAKES STAIN VIRTUALLY INVISIBLE

I   ATTEMPTS   TO   WRITE:

- WHERE   ARE   YOU   GOING ?
- I'M   GOING   TO   THE   BILLY   WOODS
- AND   WHAT   WILL   YOU   DO   THERE ?
- I   WANT   TO   SEE   IF   ANYTHING   HAS   CHANGED
- HOW   SO ?
- I   WANT   TO   SEE   IF   THE   STRUCTURE   IS   STILL   THERE
- WHAT   STRUCTURE ?
- THE   STRUCTURE   THAT   MYSELF   AND   ALAN   BUILT   SOME   YEARS   PREVIOUS
- WHO   IS   THIS   ALAN ?
- ALAN   TASTIC   WAS   A   FRIEND   OF   MINE   FROM   THE   ASYLUM. HE   IS   NOW   PERISHED   BUT   IN   THE   TIME   THAT   I   KNEW   HIM   WE   BUILT   MANY   STRUCTURES   TOGETHER   AND   DUG   MANY   HOLES. ALAN   WAS   GRAND. HE   WAS   A   METAL   FLAG   THAT   NO   WIND   COULD   GOVERN   AND   THAT'S   WHAT   I   ADMIRED   IN   HIM. THAT IS, UNTIL   THE   SINGLES   GOT   HIM.
- THERE   ARE   SINGLES   HERE   ABOUTS ?
- A   FEW   PACKS   OF   THEM. UGLY   ONES , THEIR   FACES   AS   IF   CARVED   FROM   LUMPS   OF   BOGWOOD. THEY   GOT   ALAN   SOME   TWO   YEARS   LAST   WEDNESDAY. WE   WERE   IN   OUR   DEN   AND   HAD   JUST   FINISHED   A   FINE   MEAL   OF   ROASTED   GUTS   WHEN   IN   APPEARS   A   PACK   OF   SINGLES.   THEY   HARDLY   MADE   A   SOUND   AS   THEY   ENTERED , LIKE   THE . ARM   OF   THE   BUTTERFLY. ONE   OF   THEM   HOONED   UP   TO   ALAN. SHE   WASN'T   A   STUMP   LIKE   THE   OTHERS   BUT   SPRY   AND   GREEN - TANNED   LIKE   AN   ELF. SHE   TOUCHED   HIS   OAK   AND   THAT   WAS   IT , HE   WAS   GONE.
- SOUNDS   LIKE   YOU   MISS   YOUR   ALAN   THEN ?
- AYE SO. WE   HAD   SOME   TIMES. WE   USED   TO   WEAR   SPRAY-ON   MASKS   AND   SOMETIMES   WE   DID   SHANDIES   TOGETHER. I'D   PAY   MANY   HUNDREDS   OF   SQUID   TO   GET   HIM   BACK   BUT   THERE   IT   IS.
- NEVER   MIND.
- AYE SO. MAYBE   IT'S   BEST. ~~━━━━~~   I   BUILD   SMALLER   STRUCTURES   ~~━~~ AND   DIG   SHALLOWER   HOLES   NOW   AND   PEOPLE   SEEM   TO   LIKE   THEM   MORE.

    — END —

Everyone loves a turtle

This is my granddaughter, Annabell Rose Cooper, aged three, in the Turtle outfit that I made for her. She really loves it.
Mrs M Cooper, Sheffield

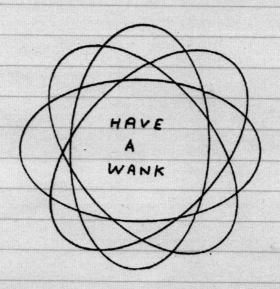

HAVE
A
WANK

MESSAGE TO EVERYONE IN THE UNIVERSE;
STOP WHAT YOU ARE DOING + LISTEN,
ONE OF GOD'S SPOKESPEOPLE IS ABOUT
TO TELL YOU ALL SOMETHING.

(150 YEARS LATER)
MAYBE NOT; GO ABOUT YOUR BUSINESS AND AWAIT FURTHER ANNOUNCEMENTS.

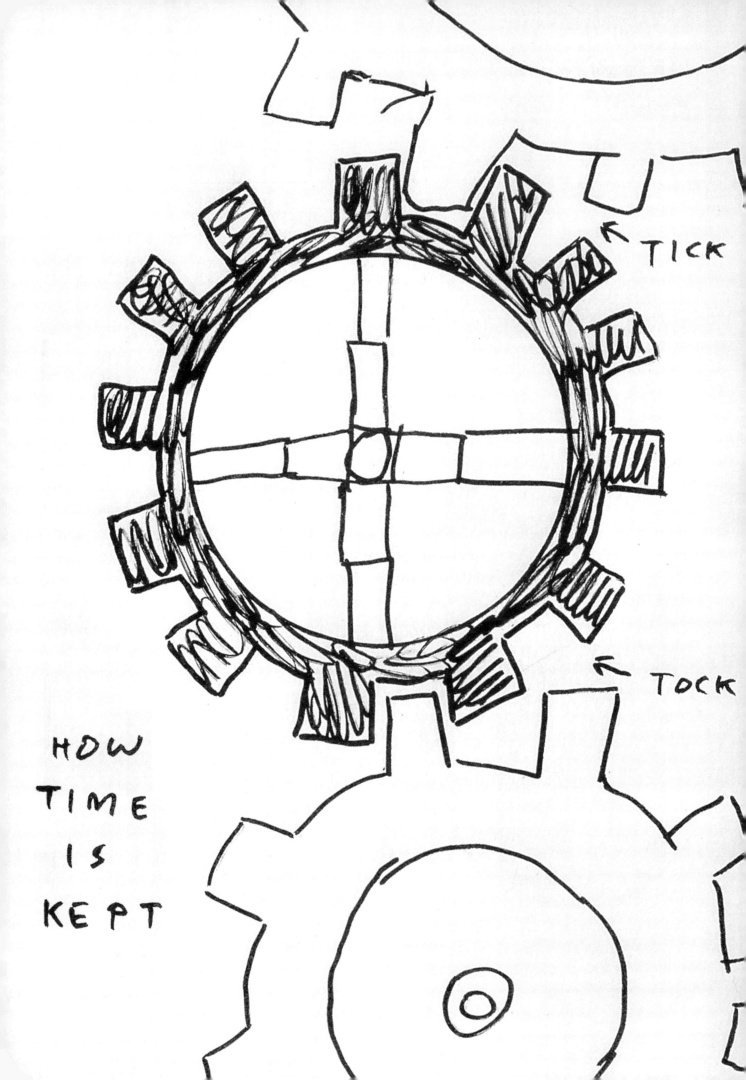

TICK

TOCK

HOW
TIME
IS
KEPT

THE LITTLE 'RED NUTS'

THEY USED TO BE KEPT IN 'THE BARN' W/OUT
SUNLIGHT BUT ARE NOW FREED DUE TO YOUR
GOODWILL AND GENEROUS DONATIONS.

THANK-YOU

PROBLEM CHILD'S VIEW OF SOCIETY

[WE ASSUME IT IS HER VIEW OF SOCIETY, THOUGH THE DRAWING COULD REPRESENT SOMETHING ELSE - IT IS IMPOSSIBLE TO ASCERTAIN AS SHE STILL REFUSES TO SPEAK TO US]

- ARE THEY GAYS ?
- NO THEY ARE NOT GAYS THEY ARE CONJOINED TWINS
- AND WILL THEY BE MADE SEPERATE ?
- YES , SOON IT WILL HAPPEN
- AND HOW ?
- A SURGEON WILL PART THEM WITH SHEARS AND THE WEAKER OF THE TWO WILL DIE
- AND WHICH ONE IS THE WEAKER ?
- THE UGLY ONE. THE BETTER-LOOKING ONE WILL SURVIVE

ART AND

DELUSION

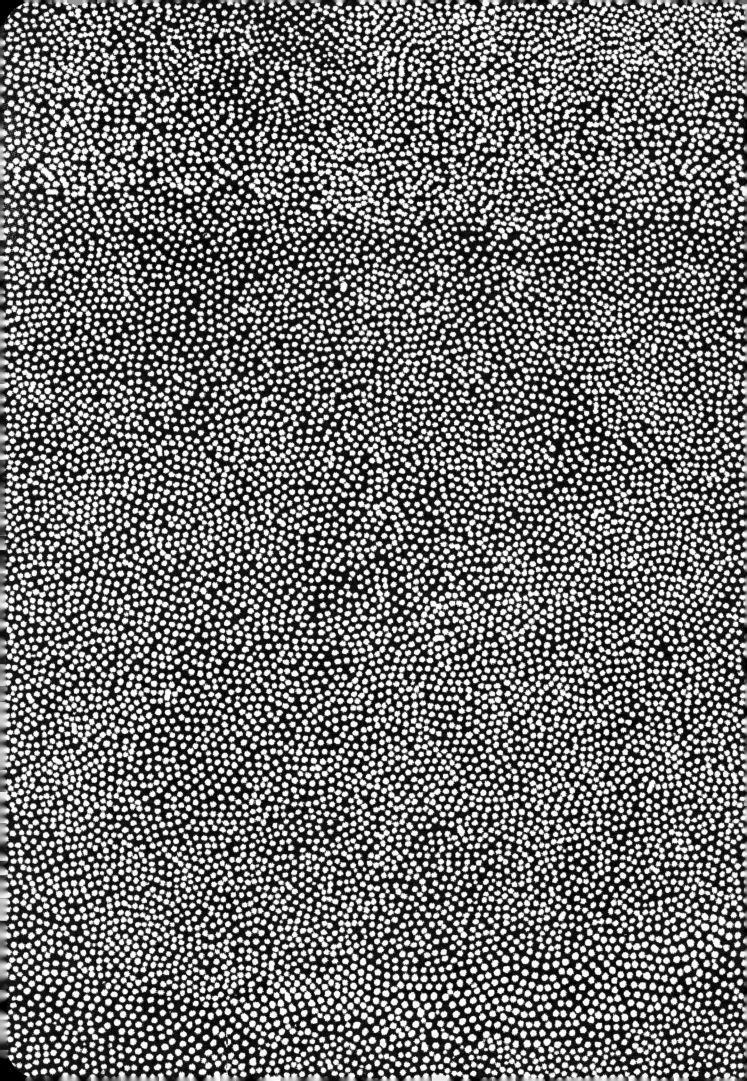

THE STUDY OF
THE HUMAN'S FORM
AND TO RENDER IT
IN CLOSE RESEMBLANCE
ON A PAGE IS THE
ARTIST'S SKILL

BUT
TO KNOW THE HEART'S
PARTICULARS AND TO
DESCRIBE THEM MOODILY
IS THE POET'S TASK

MAN SAYS: WE SHOULD STEAL THIS PAINTING
WOMAN SAYS: IF WE STEAL THIS PAINTING WE MIGHT
GET CAUGHT AND HAVE TO GO TO PRISON
MAN SAYS: I DON'T MIND
WOMAN SAYS: (NOTHING)

Movements of 'crazy dude' in Gallery. (He moves like an angry wasp)

DOG

CAT

FORTUNES TOLD

QUIET PLEASE

HAIR CUT

FLOWERS

ENTRANCE

VINEG

EXIT

ES
E ARE
PEN
AND
OSED

RM
OR
ALE

PORTAITS
PAINTED

SOUP
£1

VACANCIES
AND
NO
VACANCIES

EVERY
THING
MUST
BE
RETURNED

BOAT
RIDES

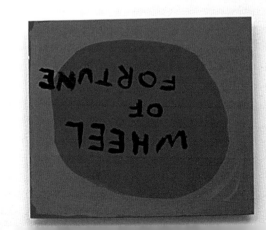

WHEEL
OF
FORTUNE

POINTLESSNESS
BOREDOM
DESPERATION
UTTER CONFUSION

35

FACES IN THE CROWD WHILE YOU WERE SPEAKING

THE
PIECE
OF
PAPER IS EXCITING

IT IS THE POTENTIAL OF THE PIECE OF PAPER THAT IS
EXCITING AS WELL
I THINK IT'S EXCITING
BUT THEN I HAVE BEEN INDOORS
FOR A LONG TIME
WITHOUT SPEAKING TO ANYONE

PICTURE DRAWN BY A DYING MAN

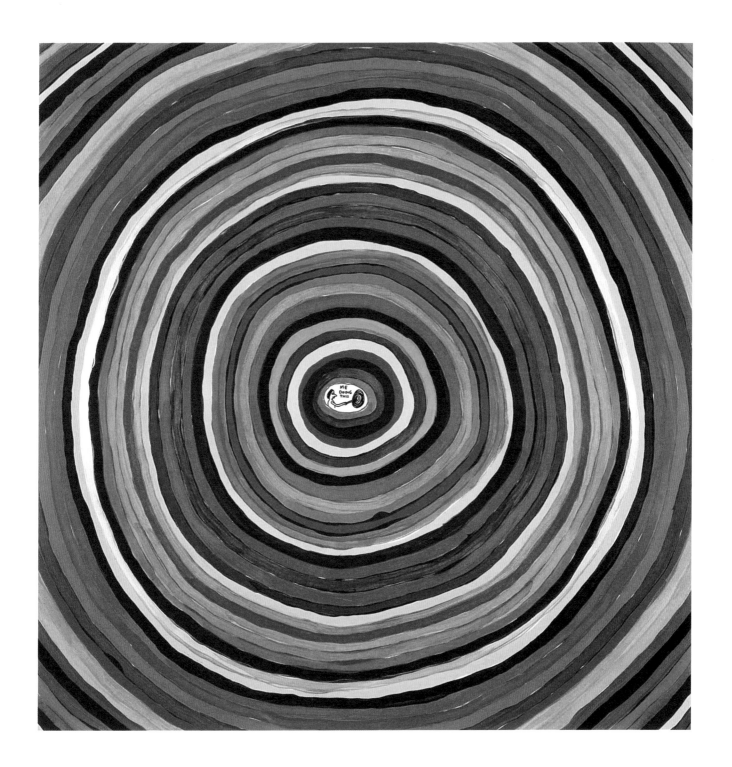

I HAVE DONE MY BEST TO REPRESENT YOU IN A FLATTERING WAY. I HAVE USED ALL MY SKILLS, OF WHICH I HAVE MANY. I HAVE DRAWN UPON MY EXHAUSTIVE STUDIES OF THE HUMAN FORM. I HAVE USED THE FINEST MATERIALS AND THE ENVIRONMENT IN WHICH I WORKED WAS PERFECT FOR SUCH A TASK.

THIS PICTURE HAS BEEN CAUSED BY A DOG'S LICKING. THE DOG HAS BEEN MADE TO LICK THE ARTIST'S WOUND AND THEN IS MADE TO LICK THE PAPER.

ON ~~SUNDAY~~ MONDAY MORNING I GOT UP AT 8 AM. FOR MY BREAKFAST I HAD 500 HARD-BOILED EGGS AND A CUP OF TEA. FOR LUNCH I HAD AN OLD CAR TYRE AND A BUCKET OF FROGS AND A~~ ~~ CARTON OF RIBENA. FOR DINNER I HAD A JAR OF ANTI-AGEING CREAM AND TWO METRES OF ELECTRIC FLEX.

ON TUESDAY I GOT UP AT ~~ ~~8 AM. FOR MY BREAKFAST I HAD A PLASTIC RULER AND NEXT DOOR'S DOG. FOR LUNCH I HAD 53 PINTS OF GUINNESS AND I WENT HOME EARLY AND WENT TO BED.

ON WEDNESDAY I GOT UP AT 3 PM. FOR 'BREAKFAST' I HAD BACON AND EGGS, 2 CUPS OF TEA AND SOME HOLIDAY BROCHURES. I DIDN'T HAVE ANY LUNCH BECAUSE IT WAS TOO LATE. FOR DINNER I ATE MY BRIEFCASE AND ALL OF MY WIFE'S CLOTHING.

ON THURSDAY I GOT UP AT 8 AM. FOR BREAKFAST I HAD A BOTTLE OF WASHING-UP LIQUID AND A CAR STEREO. FOR LUNCH I HAD THE PLUMBING FROM AN ENSUITE BATHROOM AND 2 CUPS OF TEA. FOR DINNER I ATE SOME IMPORTANT DOCUMENTS, A SKI-JACKET, A STAPLE GUN, A PAIR OF SHOES, A PACKET OF BISCUITS AND SOME ICE CREAM.

ON FRIDAY I GOT UP EARLY BECAUSE I HAD A DOCTOR'S APPOINTMENT SO I DIDN'T HAVE TIME FOR BREAKFAST. FOR LUNCH I HAD A CORNISH PASTIE AND A CUP OF TEA. FOR DINNER I ATE ALL THE PLANTS IN OUR GARDEN AND A CONCRETE PAVING SLAB.

ON SATURDAY I GOT UP AT 8 AM. (I HAVE TO WORK SATURDAYS). FOR BREAKFAST I HAD A BOWL OF MUSELI BUT I BOFFED IT UP ON MY TROUSERS. FOR LUNCH I ATE THE TROUSERS THAT I BOFFED-UP ON AND THEN I WENT TO THE BARBERS AND GOT SHAVED BALD AND I ATE ALL MY HAIR ON THE WAY BACK TO THE OFFICE. FOR DINNER I ATE AN ELECTRIC DRILL AND SOME COLESLAW.

ON SUNDAY I GOT UP AT 9 AM AND WENT TO CHURCH WITHOUT HAVING ANY BREAKFAST. FOR LUNCH I ATE A LARGE GRAVESTONE AND SOME GRASS. IN THE EVENING I WENT OUT FROM DINNER WITH MY WIFE AND I HAD SCAMPI AND SHE HAD LASAGNE.

ROUGH BEASTS

THE BEAST IS NEAR,
WE CAN SMELL HIS DAMP FUR
AND WE CAN HEAR HIS GRUNTING
AND WE CAN HEAR HIS DINNER YELPING
AND WE CAN HEAR HIS ENGINE RUNNING
WAIT A MINUTE! — IT'S NOT THE BEAST AFTER ALL!
IT'S DAD IN HIS NEW CAR! BUT WHAT'S HE DOING
OUT HERE IN THE FOREST LATE AT NIGHT?

ELEPHANTS

STARRING
2 ELEPHANTS

I MADE THIS MASK IN MY STUDIO TO HELP YOU TO LOOK SCARY. IT'S MADE FROM PAPER MACHÉ AND REAL HAIR (MINE) WITH PAINT. I SUGGEST YOU WEAR AN OVERCOAT WITH IT WITH THE COLLAR UP — THIS WILL INCREASE THE FEAR FACTOR. MAYBE YOU COULD GROWL A BIT — LISTEN TO YOUR DOG, LEARN FROM HIM.

BILL: 1, 2, 3, 4, 5, 6, 7, 8, 9, 10, 11, 12, 13, 14, 15, 16, 17, 18, 19, 20, 21, 22, ...

BEN: STOP!

BILL: 23, 24, 25, 26, 27 ....

BEN: I SAID STOP!

BILL: 28, 29, 30 ....

BEN: STOP IT AT ONCE!

BILL: 31, 32, 33 ....

BEN: STOP IT NOW!

BILL: WHY?

BEN: IT MAKES ME UNHAPPY

BILL: WHY DOES IT MAKE YOU UNHAPPY?

BEN: BECAUSE MY LAST BOYFRIEND USED TO DO THAT AND HE TRIED TO STRANGLE ME WHILE I WAS ASLEEP

- END-

A PIRATE

ARTIST
EATEN BY
A WOLF

MEDICAL MATTERS

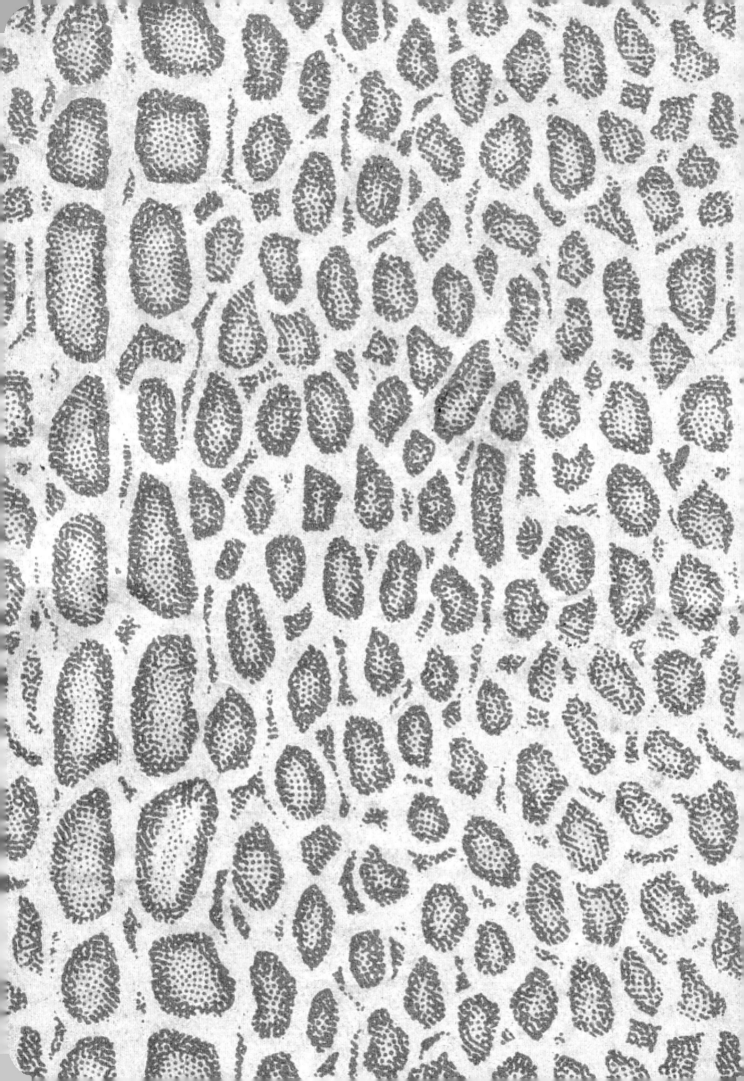

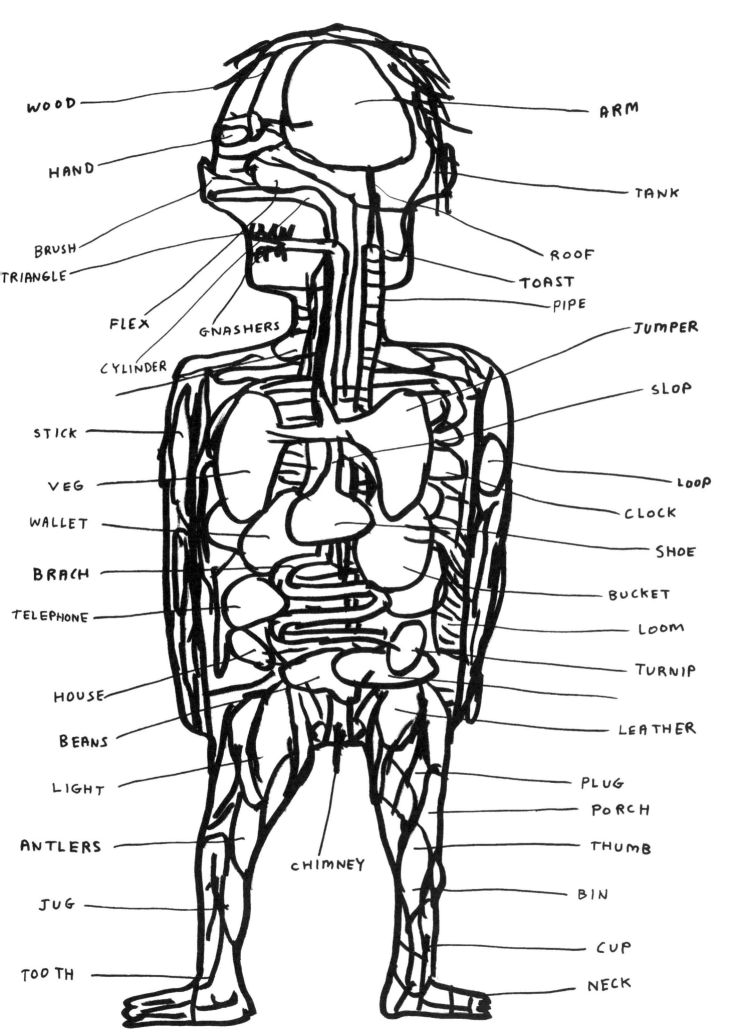

WOOD

HAND

BRUSH

TRIANGLE

FLEX

GNASHERS

CYLINDER

STICK

VEG

WALLET

BRACH

TELEPHONE

HOUSE

BEANS

LIGHT

ANTLERS

JUG

TOOTH

CHIMNEY

ARM

TANK

ROOF

TOAST

PIPE

JUMPER

SLOP

LOOP

CLOCK

SHOE

BUCKET

LOOM

TURNIP

LEATHER

PLUG

PORCH

THUMB

BIN

CUP

NECK

59

THE DOCTORS

THEY REMOVED HIS SPIT█ GLAND

THEY LISTENED TO THE SPARROWS BREAST

THEY TORCHED THE GARMENT DISTRICT TO KILL THE ██ MOTHS

THEY OPERATED ON HIS HEAD AND TOOK OUT HIS BRAIN

AND WHEN THEY TRIED TO PUT IT BACK IT WOULD NOT FIT

THEY BROKE THE LIFE SUPPORT MACHINE

THEY HARASS THE GOOD, KIND NURSES

THEY ALL SMOKE AND DRIVE SPORTS CARS AT 100 MPH.

THEY NEVER WASH THEIR HANDS

THEY STUDIED FOR MANY YEARS AND THEY WILL NOT LET US FORGET
                                                          IT.

THEY PLAYED RUGBY WITH A HUMAN SKULL (WHEN THEY WERE AT
                                                   COLLEGE)

THEY FILL SYRINGES WITH ██████

THEY PLAY GOLF

THEY ████ TATTOO SWEARWORDS ON INTERNAL ORGANS DURING OPERATIONS

THEY DO NOT WANT US TO HEAL, NOT FULLY

THEY MESS WITH MEDICAL DATABASES

THEY DO NOT KNOW THE MEANING OF THE WORD 'STERILE'

THEY DRINK WHISKEY FROM TEST TUBES

THEY BLOW HORNS, WHISTLES, RING BELLS, SHOUT LATE AT NIGHT, NAKED.

THEY BANG DRUMS WITH FIBULAS

THEY PLAY ROUNDERS WITH TIBIAS

THEY BREAK WINDOWS WITH FEMURS

THEY UNBLOCK THE TOILET WITH A HUMERUS

THEY MIX DRINKS WITH METACARPALS

THEY FIGHT WITH DENTISTS

THEY LABOTOMIZE THOSE WHO COMPLAIN

THEY BRANDISH SCALPELS LIKE SWORDS

THEY EAT MEAT FROM THE CORPSES BELIEVING IT WILL MAKE THEM STRONG

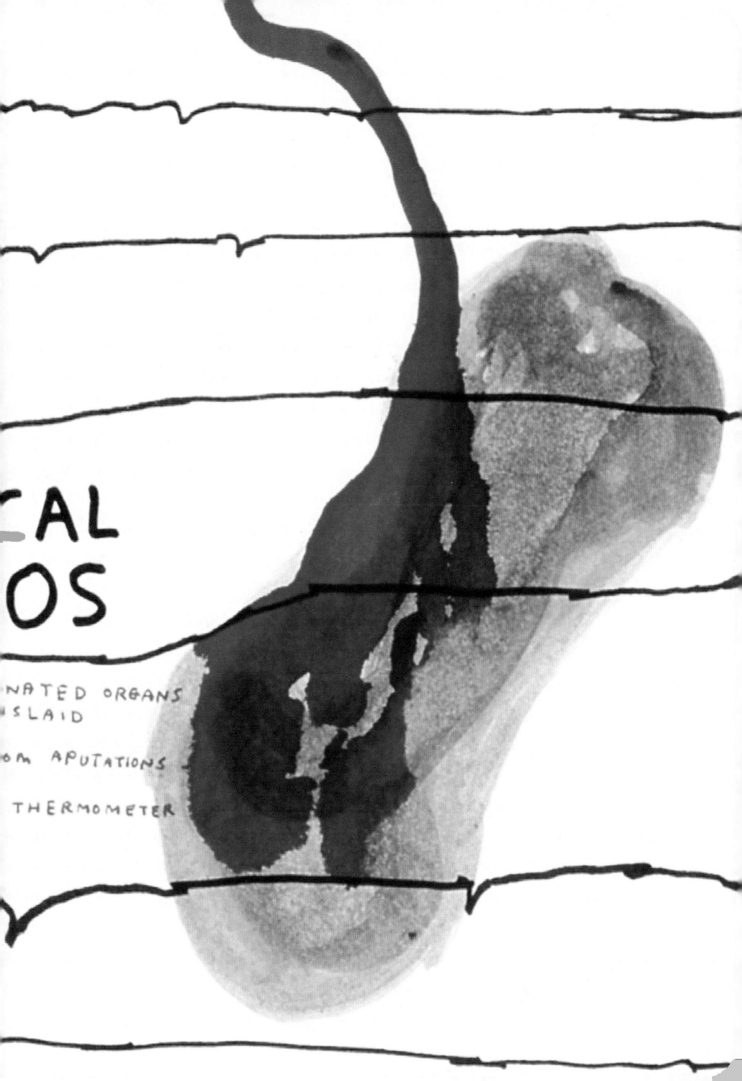

CAL

OS

NATED ORGANS
SLAID

om APUTATIONS

THERMOMETER

AT THE HOSPITAL

- THEY HAVE RUN OUT OF DNA.
- THEY CUT OFF BAD LIMBS AND BURN THEM AND REPLACE THEM WITH PLASTIC ████ PARTS.
- YOU CAN'T GET IN UNLESS YOU'RE SICK OR UNLESS YOU KNOW SOMEONE IN THERE THAT'S SICK.
- YOU CAN'T PARK OUTSIDE.
- THE TOPS OF THE CABINETS ARE COVERED IN DIRT.
- YOU ARE LIABLE TO BE KEPT WAITING FOR MANY HOURS DURING WHICH TIME YOU WILL CONTRACT A DRUG-RESISTANT PLAGUE
- THEY STICK TUBES UP YOU AND FILL YOU UP WITH GREY FLUID.
- THEY PRETEND THAT DEAD PEOPLE ARE STILL ALIVE.
- YOU HAVE TO LEAVE YOUR DIGNITY AT THE DOOR.
- THEY TAKE X-RAYS OF YOU BUT THEY PAY NO ATTENTION TO THEM, THEY MIGHT ASWELL DO DRAWINGS OF WHAT THEY THINK IS INSIDE YOU.
- THEY NEVER ANSWER THE TELEPHONE.
- THEY ENCOURAGE PATIENTS TO BRAWL WITH EACH OTHER.
- THE MORTUARY SLAB AWAITS US ALL.
- NO ONE IS QUALIFIED.
- THE NURSES DRINK BLOOD.
- THE LIFE SUPPORT MACHINE IS 'ON THE BLINK'.
- THEY TURN A BLIND EYE TO THOSE WHO STEAL NEWBORN BABIES

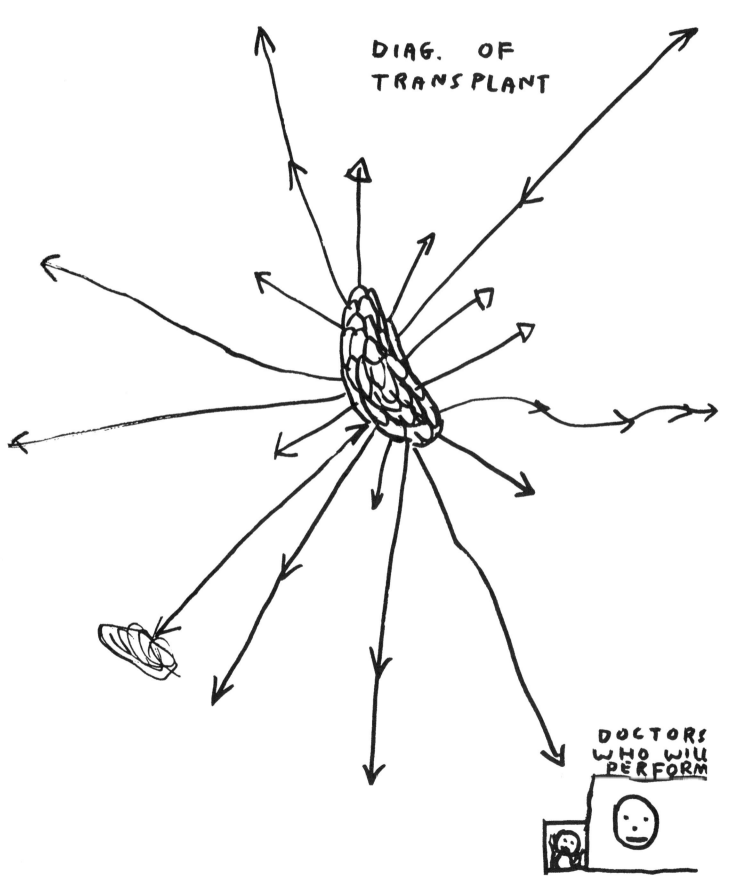

DIAG. OF TRANSPLANT

DOCTORS WHO WILL PERFORM

MIGRAINE

TOOTHACHE

HEAVY FALL

MENTAL ILL

AND DRY SCALP

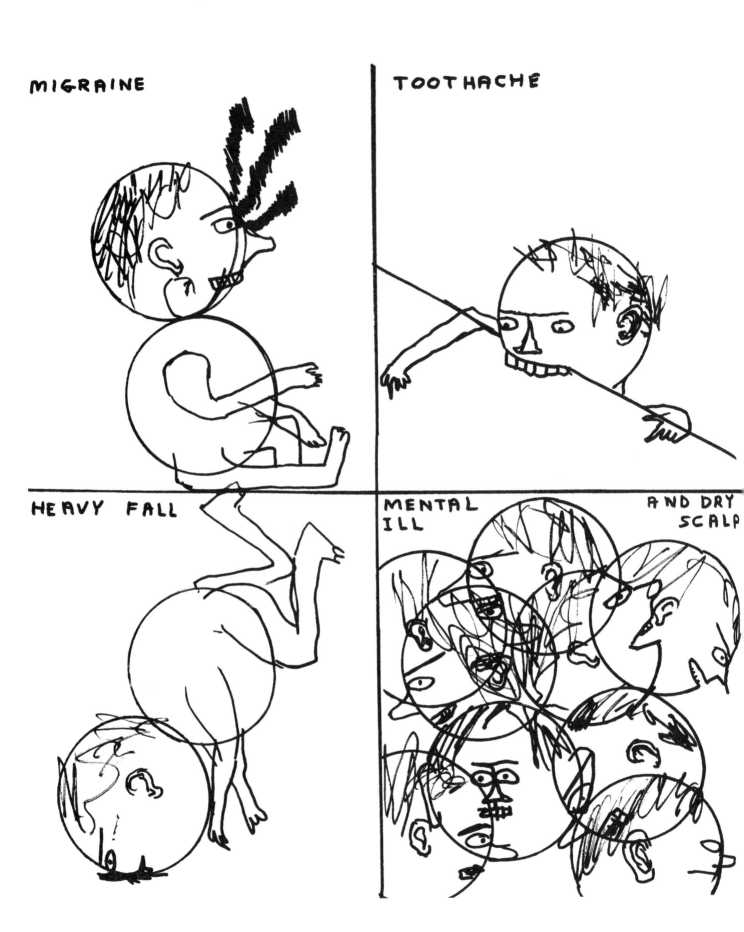

FATHER & SON

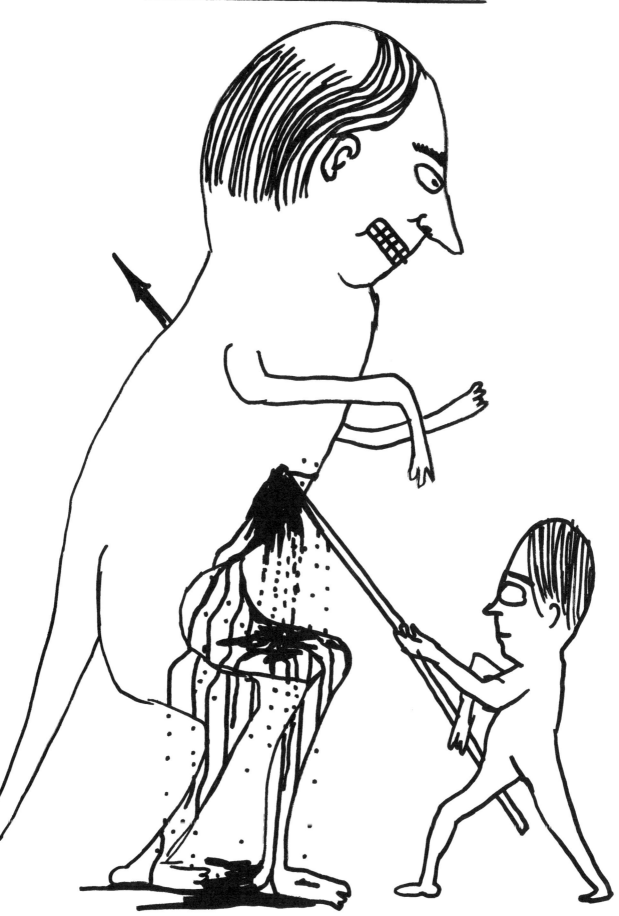

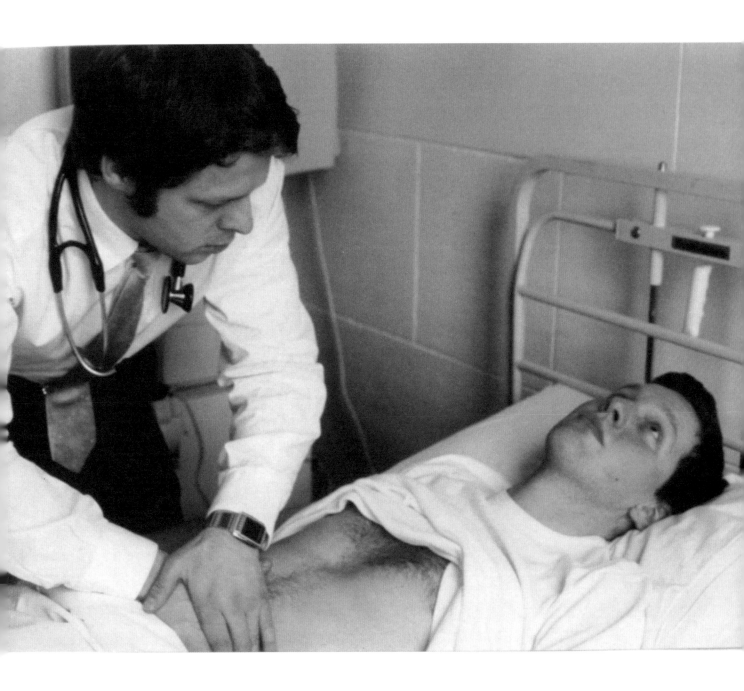

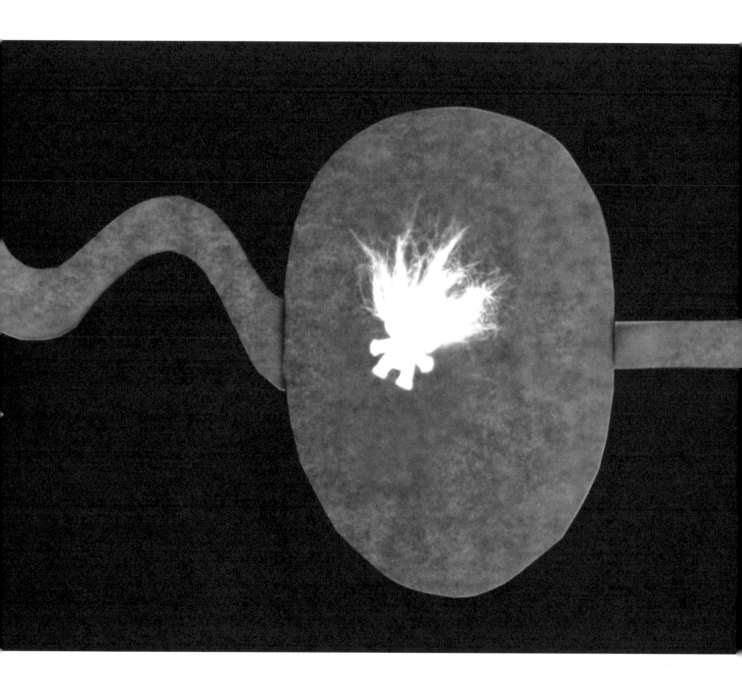

ME NEXT PLEASE

I CAN'T WAIT ANY LONGER

I WANT TO SEE THE PSYCHIATRIC DOCTOR RIGHT NOW

CATASTROPHES AND OTHER EVERYDAY EVENTS

FAMILY PHOTOS
(TORN & DISCARDED)
LIVES RUINED
PETS LOST
HOUSES BURNED

THIS DRAWING REJECTED BY KIDDIES COMIC

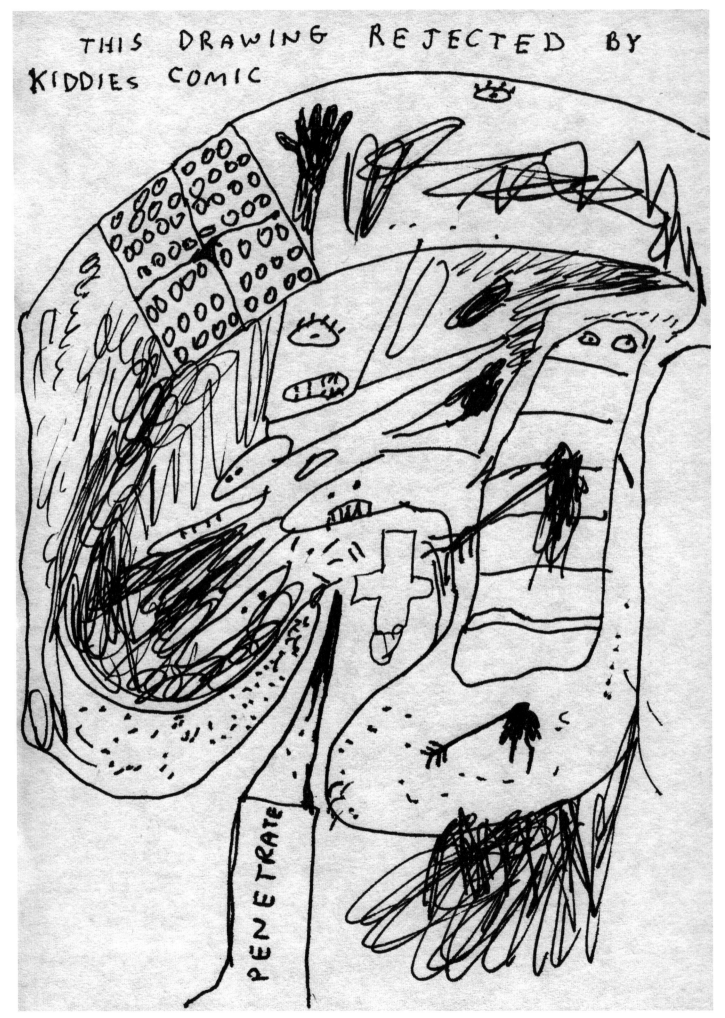

PENETRATE

LADY CONNIE FEATHERBRIDGE, SEVERELY BITTEN BY A CROCODILE, WEARING A BROWN SUEDE TUNIC, BELGIAN CONGO, 1887.

MAJOR SMETHWICK-BROWN, EATEN BY A CROCODILE, INDIA, 1892.

A WEIRD DAY THING HAPPENED

TO THE OTHER ME

SHORT, SHARP SHOCK

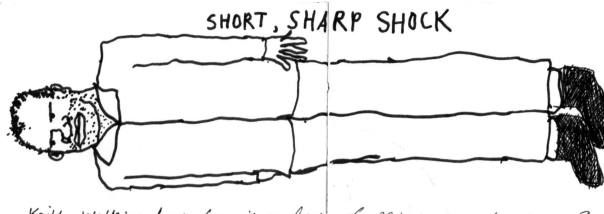

Keith Watkins has been in and out of prison since he was 9 years old. This evening he received a SHORT, SHARP SHOCK when he returned home to find his mother wearing his underwear and listening to his Clash records. He strangled her with a pair of his enormous Y-fronted underpants. With his huge, fat Arse bared, he then telephoned the police.

ZING

77

NO
SPEED
LIMIT
ANYMORE
GO AS FAST AS YOU
WANT — LIKE IN
GERMANY

WE WENT ON HOLIDAY TO ITALY

IT WAS SHITE,
THE PLANE CRASHED
AND WE ALL GOT KILLED

HAIR

WITHOUT HAIR, THERE WOULD
BE NO SHAMPOO. WIGS WOULD
BE VERY DIFFERENT, UNRECOGNIS-
ABLE FROM WHAT THEY ARE TODAY.
SONG TITLES AND LYRICS WOULD
HAVE TO BE CHANGED. HEAD-LICE
WOULD BE LIKE THE MONKIES
IN THE RAINFOREST AFTER THE
WOODSMEN HAVE CUT DOWN
THE TREES.

DOWN THE MINES MORALE IS LOW

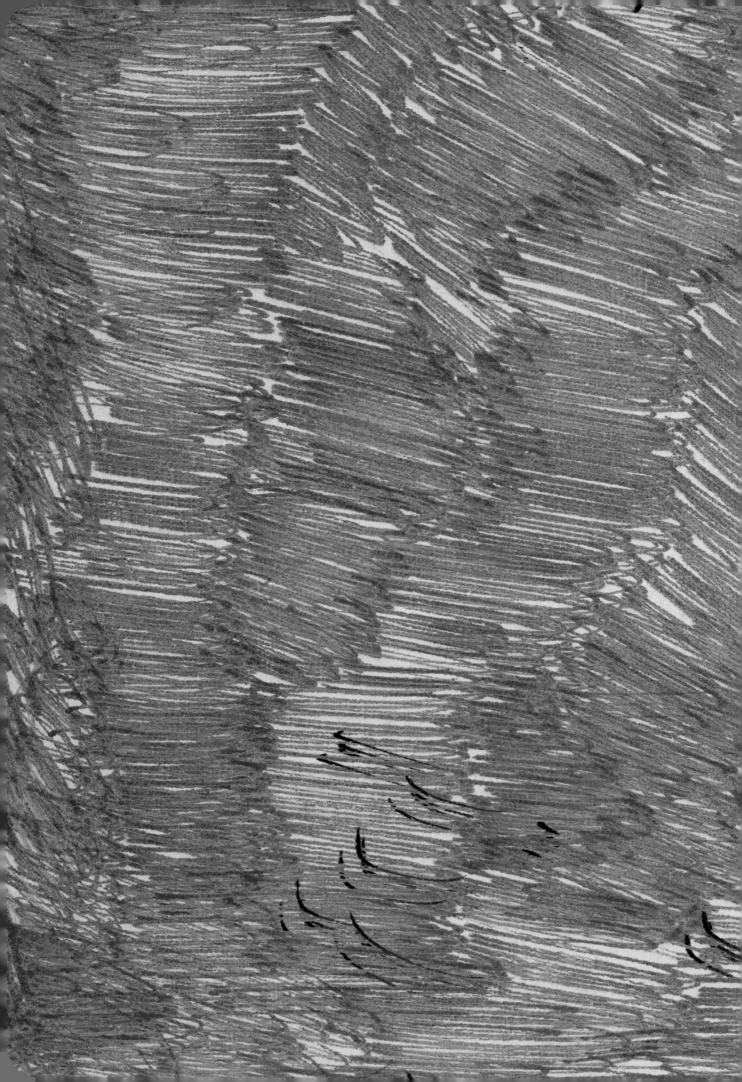

THESE PAGES HAVE NO NUMBERS

EG: 1, 2, 3, 4, ETC.

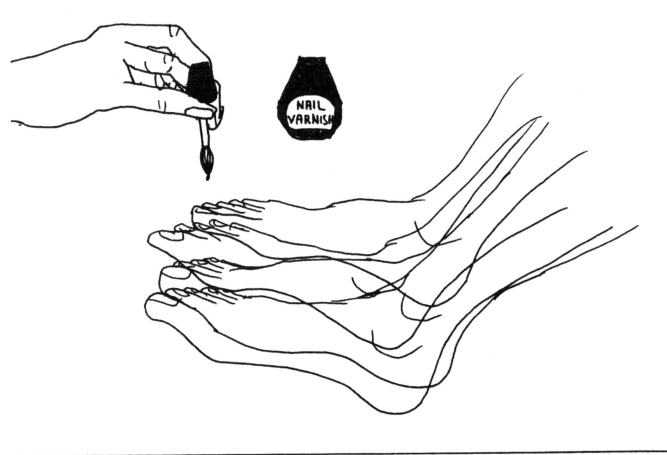

SEIZURE AT THE ~~THE~~ BEAUTY ~~PARLOR~~ PARLOUR

MISSING
SINCE
THURSDAY

HAVE YOU SEEN THEM?
CALL POLICE

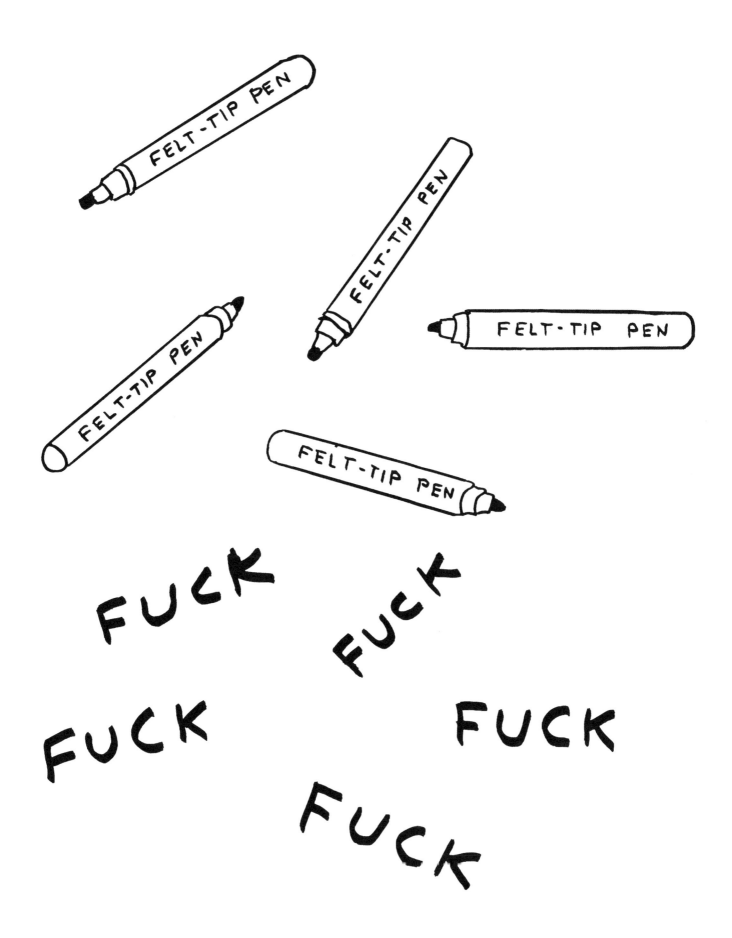

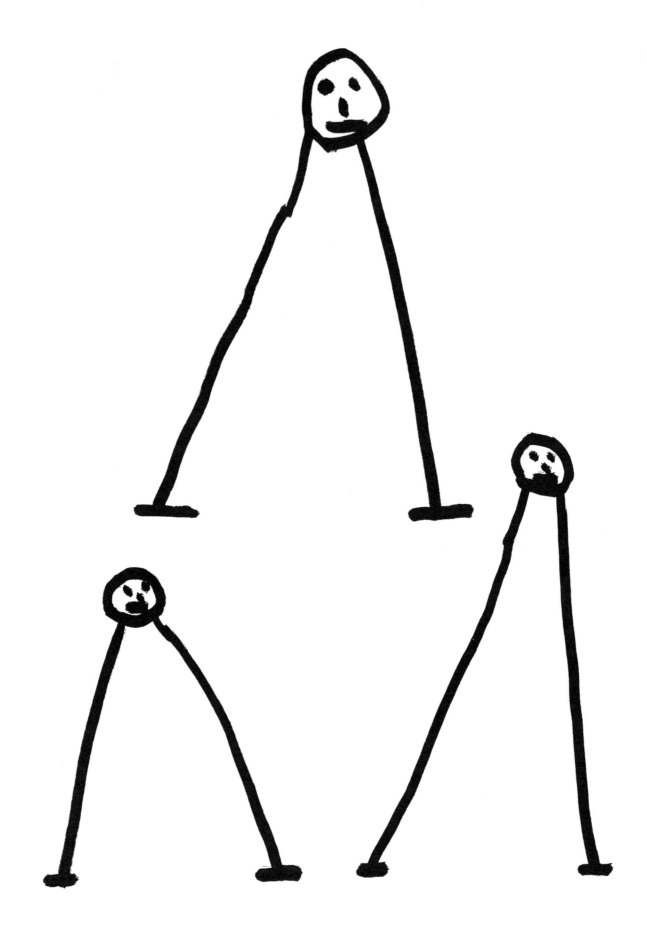

STATEMENT: FROG
QUESTION: LUMINOUS FROG?
ANSWER: NO, DULL FROG

S: SPOON
Q: CONVENTIONAL SPOON?
A: YES

S: ASS - CANDY
Q: HORSE'S ASS - CANDY?
A: NO, SOUR ASS - CANDY

S: ONE POUND COIN
Q: ONE POUND COIN WITH SHARPENED EDGES?
A: YES

S: ATTENTION TO DETAIL
Q: NORMAL ATTENTION TO DETAIL?
A: NO, SUB-STANDARD

S: EGG
Q: DRILLED EGG?
A: YES

S: JUMP LEADS
Q: JUMP LEADS FOR A CAR?
A: NO JUMP LEADS FOR A HEART ATTACK. TO BRING HIM BACK
                                                    TO LIFE

S: SPIDERS
Q: SPIDERS THE SIZE OF MEN?
A: YES

HIGH TIDE :

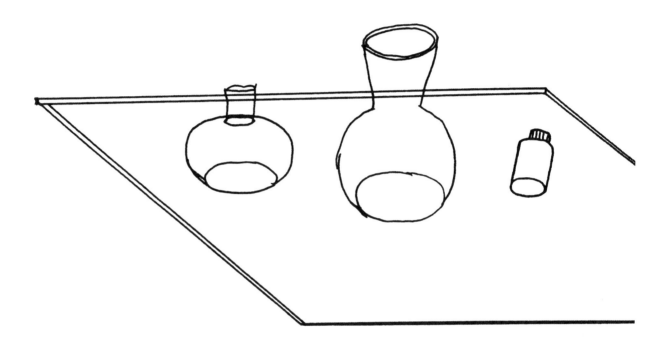

GLASS SHELF

I SMOKE CANNABIS
AND LOOK ^{UP} AT IT FOR HOURS

MY STRUGGLE

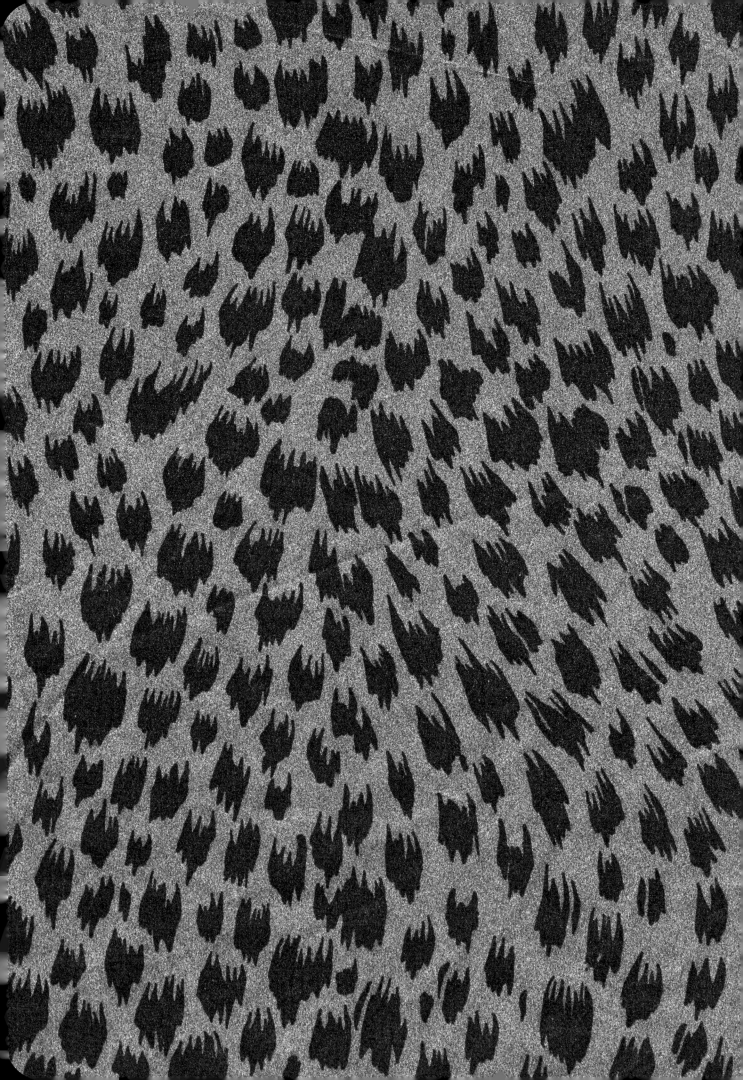

THE FIRST PAGE

THE FIRST PAGE IS ALWAYS THE MOST DIFFICULT TO WRITE. THE LAST PAGE CAN ALSO BE DIFFICULT, BUT NOT AS DIFFICULT AS THE FIRST.

THE SECOND PAGE IS EASY TO WRITE WHEN COMPARED WITH THE FIRST PAGE. THE SECOND PAGE IS USUALLY MORE EASY TO WRITE THAN THE LAST, THOUGH NOT ALWAYS.

NEVER TRUST THOSE WHO ARE
SCARRED AND DISFIGURED THEY
ARE ALL THIEVES AND MURDERERS

NEVER TRUST THOSE WITH BEADY
EYES THEY WILL ALSO STEAL
FROM YOU.

YOU CAN TRUST PEOPLE WITH
BEARDS BECAUSE THEY'RE LIKE
JESUS OR GOD.

NEVER TRUST PEOPLE WHO
ARE REALLY SHORT, NOT LIKE
SMALL BUT REALLY SHORT
BECAUSE THEY ARE IN LEAGUE
WITH THE DEVIL.

NEVER TRUST THOSE WHO
ARE OVERLY POLITE, YOU
SHOULD KILL THEM IF YOU
GET THE CHANCE.

I am good

I am good | I am good

I am good | I am C

I am | I am y

I am good | I am good

i am good | I am good

I am good | I am good

101

DELIVERED TO YOUR DOOR

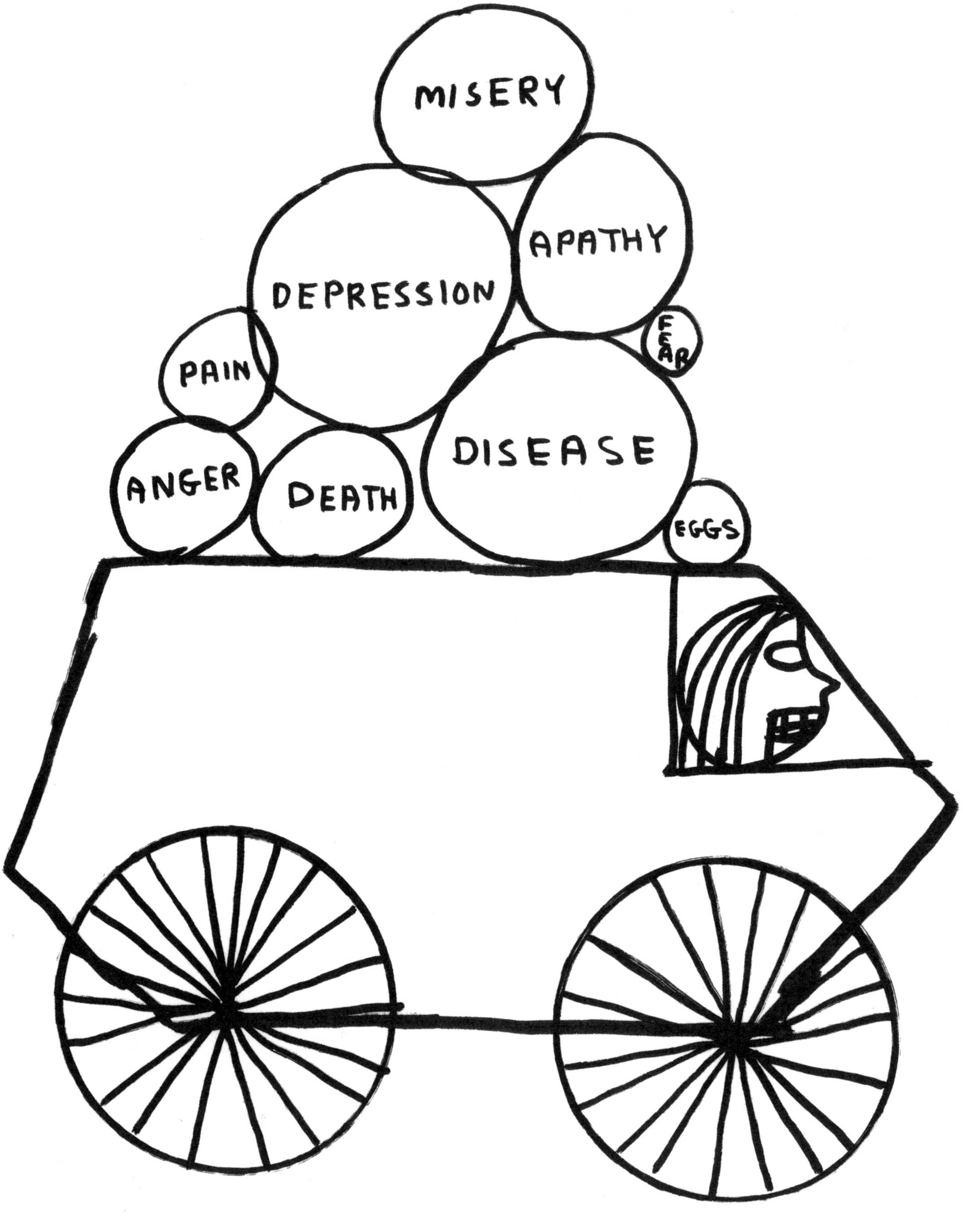

MISERY

APATHY

DEPRESSION

PAIN

FEAR

ANGER

DEATH

DISEASE

EGGS

IT HAS ALWAYS
BEEN MY
DESIRE TO
WRITE POETRY
BUT I FIND
IT INCREDIBLY
FUCKING DIFFICULT

DON'T DRINK THE GREY WINE
IT TASTES AS WATER FROM THE CANAL DOES
SEE, I HAVE DRANK A HALF-GALLON

FROM NOW ON
I WILL DO
EXACTLY
AS I AM TOLD

BUT I WILL NOT DO ANYTHING THAT IS AGAINST THE LAW
AND I WILL NOT REMOVE ANY PART OF MY CLOTHING
AND I WILL NOT DO ANYTHING SEXUAL
AND I WILL NOT DO ANYTHING AT NIGHT TIME (AFTER 5 PM)
AND I WILL NOT DO ANYTHING OUTDOORS IF IT IS RAINING
AND I WILL NOT DO ANYTHING OUT OF TOWN
AND I WILL NOT DO ANYTHING IN THE ROUGH PARTS OF TOWN
AND I WOULD RATHER NOT DO ANYTHING WITH RETARDED PEOPLE OR DISABLED PEOPLE OR CHILDREN OR ANIMALS
AND I WOULD RATHER NOT DO ANYTHING WITH FOREIGN PEOPLE OR PEOPLE WITH STRONG REGIONAL ACCENTS
AND I WILL NOT DO ANYTHING NEAR LARGE BODIES OF WATER
AND I WILL NOT DO ANYTHING DOWN MINES
AND I WILL NOT DO ANYTHING DOWN THE SEWER OR NEAR TO DRAINS
AND I WILL NOT DO ANYTHING WHERE THERE IS DUST OR DIRT OR INSECTS OR SMELLS
AND I WILL NOT DO ANYTHING EARLY IN THE MORNING
AND I WILL NOT DO ANYTHING IN WINTER
AND I WILL NOT DO ANYTHING IF YOU SHOUT AT ME
AND I WILL NOT DO ANYTHING IF YOU CALL ME WHAT YOU CALLED ME IN YOUR PAMPHLET
AND I WILL NOT DO ANYTHING BORING
AND I WILL NOT DO ANYTHING OBVIOUS OR TRITE OR BANAL
AND I WILL NOT DO ANYTHING DANGEROUS
AND I WILL NOT TAKE ANY PILLS
AND I MUST BE ABLE TO SMOKE CIGARETTES
AND I WILL NOT READ ANYTHING
AND I WILL NOT SAY ANYTHING
AND I WILL NOT DO ANYTHING DEPRESSING
AND I WILL NOT RENOUNCE MY BEHAVIOUR PREVIOUS TO THIS RESOLUTION
AND I WILL NOT ENDORSE YOUR OPINIONS (ESPECIALLY YOUR OPINIONS ABOUT ME)
AND I WILL NOT SIGN ANYTHING (EXCEPT THIS)
AND I WILL NOT. WRITE ANYTHING (EXCEPT THIS)
AND I MUST BE ABLE TO WEAR MY OWN CLOTHES
BUT APART FROM THESE THINGS YOU CAN CONSIDER ME YOUR HUMBLE AND LOYAL SERVANT
AND I WOULD LIKE TO TAKE THIS OPPORTUNITY TO THANK YOU FOR YOUR KIND OFFER OF EMPLOYMENT AND
I SINCERELY HOPE THAT I CAN LIVE UP TO YOUR CONFIDENCE IN ME.
GOD BLESS YOU KIND SIR.
I LOVE YOU.

MY

ONLY

FAILING

IS MY

TERRIBL

ARRAGNCE

THE KNOT

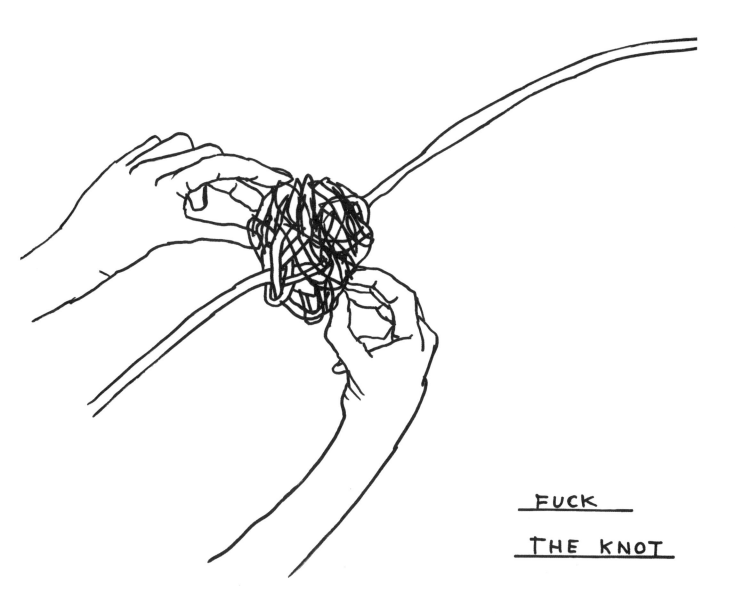

FUCK

THE KNOT

I KEEP
KNOCKING
THINGS OVER
I CAN'T
HELP IT
I'M
CLUMBSY
LIKE AN
~~████~~ ~~████████~~
ELEPHANT

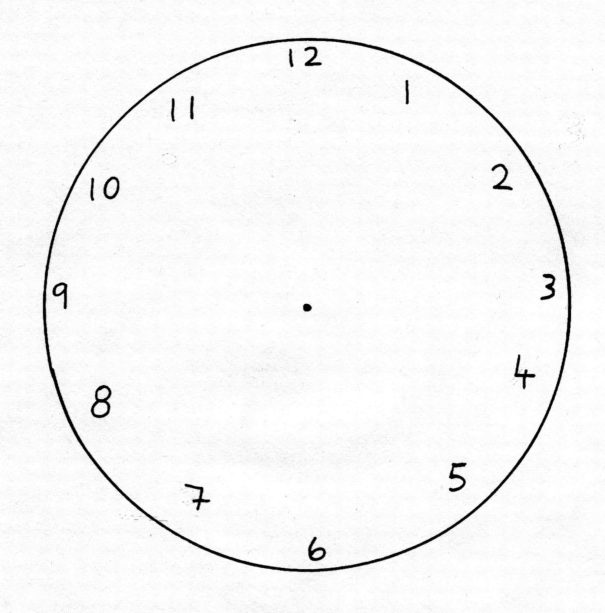

Q. WHAT TIME IS IT ?

A. I DON'T KNOW

FEAR

THE THINGS THAT WE ARE
NOT AFRAID OF ARE THE
MOST DANGEROUS

Weakness

IT IS IN YOUR WEAKNESS THAT
I FIND STRENGTH

ANGER

BECAUSE NOTHING IS RELEVENT

BLANK SCREEN

LETTERBOX MODE

I DON'T LIKE LETTERBOX MODE
IT GIVES ME HEADACHES

OF THOSE MARKS BELOW:

MOST OF THE MARKS WERE MADE
IN HASTE

A FEW WERE MADE WITH
CARE

ALL OF THE MARKS WERE
MADE IN ANGER

ALL OF THE MARKS WERE
MADE WITH THE SAME PEN
AND THAT'S ALL I CAN SAY
ABOUT THEM

The end of civilization

THE END OF CIVILIZATION
CAN'T COME SOON ENOUGH
AS FAR AS I'M CONCERNED

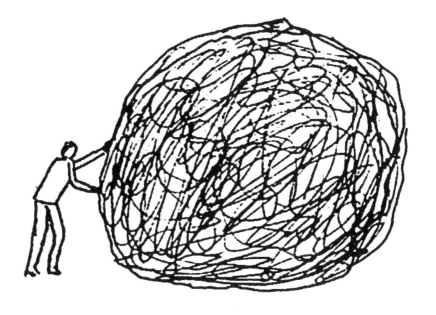

HARD

WORK

THE MORE ANGRIER WHAT I GET
THE MORE WHAT I GET DONE

~~THE MORE WHAT I GET DONE~~

THE MORE WHAT I GET DONE
IT MAKES ME ANGRIER
AND ●● ON AND SO ON

As I go up the steps
to receive my award
I wave to freinds and
family in the crowd

TWAT

YOU'RE A
TWAT

YOU TWAT

TWAT

PICK UP THE PEN
PUT DOWN THE PEN
PICK UP THE PEN
PUT DOWN THE PEN
PICK UP THE PEN
PUT DOWN THE PEN
PICK UP THE PEN
PUT DOWN THE PEN
PICK UP THE PEN
PUT DOWN THE PEN
PICK UP THE PEN
PUT DOWN THE PEN
PICK UP THE PEN
PUT DOWN THE PEN
PICK UP THE PEN
PUT DOWN THE PEN
PICK UP THE PEN
PUT DOWN THE PEN
PICK UP THE PEN
PUT DOWN THE PEN
PICK UP THE PEN
PUT DOWN THE PEN
PICK UP THE PEN
PUT DOWN THE PEN

DEAR DAVID SHRIGLEY,

AFTER READING A FEW OF YOUR BOOKS AND LOOKING AT SOME OF YOUR SCULPTURES OVER THE INTERNET I HAVE DECIDED THAT I WOULD LIKE TO BE YOUR ASSISTANT. I AM INTERESTED HOW SUCH A MAN AS YOURSELF GOES ABOUT HIS DAILY BUSINESS, AS AN ARTIST AND I AM INTERESTED IN ASSISTING YOU GO ABOUT YOUR DAILY BUSINESS. I KNOW I WOULD GREATLY BENEFIT FROM THIS EXPERIANCE AS I AM CURRENTLY IN MY SECOND YEAR AT CHELSEA COLLEGE OF ART AND DESIGN STUDYING ON A FINE ART BA COURSE. THANK YOU FOR TAKING THE TIME TO READ THIS LETTER AND HOPEFULLY WE SHALL BE IN TOUCH IN THE FUTURE.

SINCERELY,

PETE DONALDSON

P.S.
I UNDERSTAND IN A FEW WEEKS YOU SHALL BE LECTURING HERE, SO MAYBE THEN WE COULD HAVE A CHAT. THANKS,

PETE

MY EMAIL ADDRESS IS █████████████
MY MOBILE IS: █████████████

DO NOT ENTER MY

PERSONAL SPACE

YOU ARE NOT WELCOME

SINCE YOUR PRESENCE

INTERFERES WITH MY

LIFESTYLE

AND GIVES ME A HEADACHE

WHAT DO YOU THINK OF HER?
SHE CERTAINLY IS!
DO YOU THINK SHE'S UP FOR IT?
UP FOR GOING DANCING WITH A
PAIR OF ROGUES SUCH AS WE?
NO?

I THINK SHE'S GORGEOUS
SHE CERTAINLY IS
UP FOR WHAT?
NO.

NO, SHE DOESN'T LOOK LIKE
THAT SORT OF GIRL.

THE BEST ~~██████~~ I EVER HAD

THE BEST ~~█████~~ I EVER HAD WAS WITH ~~█████~~ ~~████████~~ ON THE ~~████~~ OF ~~████████~~ 19~~███~~ . WE DID IT ~~█████~~ ~~█████~~ ~~███~~ ~~████~~ ~~███████~~ AND IT LASTED FOR ~~████~~ ~~█████████~~ . IT WAS REALLY GREAT AND I REMEMBER IT VIVIDLY EVEN NOW

FOUNDATIONS

SOMETIMES WHEN I AM IN MY PARENTS HOUSE (THE HOUSE WHERE I GREW UP) I THINK ABOUT THE FOUNDATION, ON ITS OWN WITHOUT THE HOUSE, JUST A BIG SLAB OF CONCRETE. IT WOULD BE GOOD FOR PLAYING TENNIS ON.

SOMETIMES WHEN I AM WITH THE BEAUTIFUL ONE (THE ONE WHOM I HAVE LOVED ALWAYS) I THINK ABOUT HER ON HER OWN WITHOUT HER BOYFREIND, JUST A GIRL IN THE PUB. WE COULD PLAY TENNIS TOGETHER ON THE FOUNDATIONS OF MY PARENTS HOUSE.

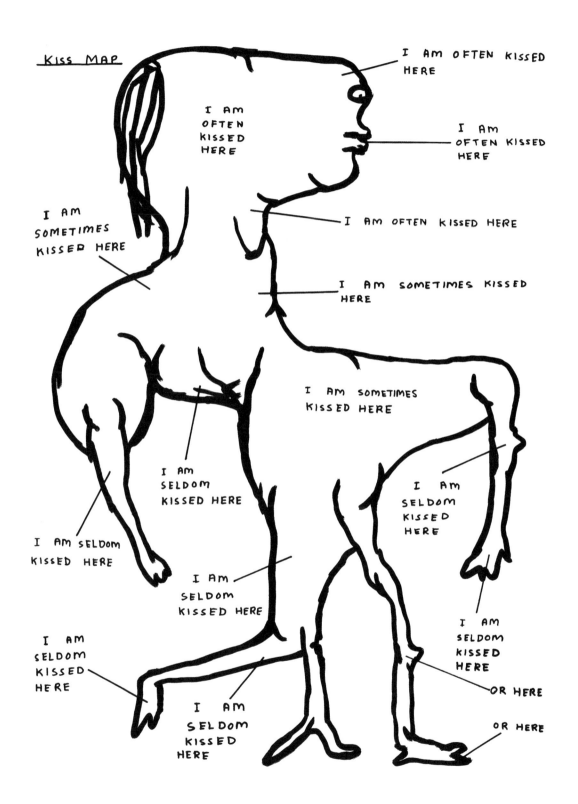

BEAST THAT YOU ARE
3 ARMS THAT YOU HAVE TO HOLD ME
4 HANDS TO TOUCH ME WITH
ONE EYE TO GAZE UPON ME

ONE LEG
A PROBOSIS ON YOUR LOWER ABDOMEN
NO HEAD AS SUCH
AND A TUFT OF COARSE HAIR ON YOUR CHEST
YOU ARE PERFECT
MY DARLING

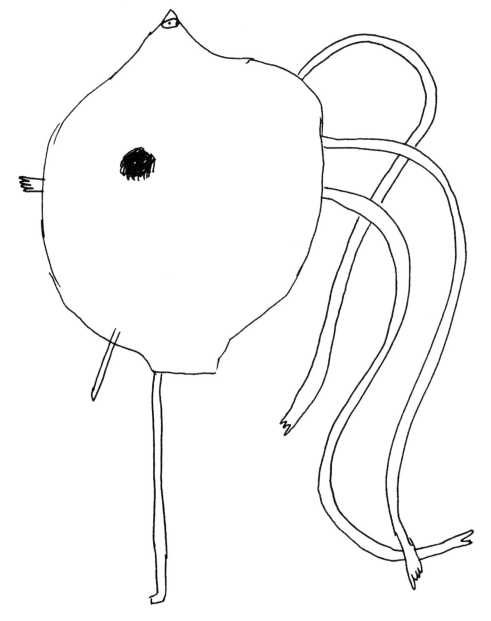

126

PROSTITUTE

CLIENT

THIS IS TO TELL YOU ABOUT THE BARN DANCE

IT IS ON SUNDAY AT 8 PM IN THE BARN

AT THE KNOCKING SHOP:

1ST WHORE: WHERE HAVE YOU BEEN ?

2ND WHORE: I'VE BEEN FOR A JOB INTERVIEW

1ST WHORE: WHAT WAS THE JOB?

2ND WHORE: PSYCHIATRIST

1ST WHORE: WHAT DO YOU WANT TO BE A PSYCHIATRIST FOR ? YOU'D HAVE TO SPEND ALL DAY TALKING TO NUT-JOBS WHICH I IMAGINE WOULD BE QUITE TEDIOUS

2ND WHORE: ACTUALLY, I THINK I WOULD RATHER ENJOY IT. I HAVE ALWAYS BEEN FASCINATED BY THE BEHAVIOUR OF THE ~~████~~ EMOTIONALLY UNKEMPT

1ST WHORE: OH, I SEE. DID YOU GET THE JOB ?

2ND WHORE: NO

— END —

HOMOSEXUAL

SACKED FROM SAINSBURYS

THE DEVIL FINDS WORK FOR
IDLE HANDS. TO RETURN THE
FAVOUR (WE PRESUME) IDLE HANDS
GIVES DEVIL A ~~____~~ HAND-JOB
IN SAINSBURYS CAR-PARK. THEY
ARE CAUGHT BY POLICE. DEVIL
ESCAPES WITH A CAUTION ~~____~~ (IT
~~__~~ IS HIS FIRST OFFENCE) BUT
IDLE HANDS HAS BEEN CAUGHT DOING
STUFF BEFORE AND GETS 40 HOURS
COMMUNITY SERVICE. HE IS MADE
TO SWEEP UP LEAVES AND PAINT
THE RAILINGS AROUND THE PARK.
"IT COULD HAVE BEEN WORSE"
HIS LAWYER TELLS HIM.

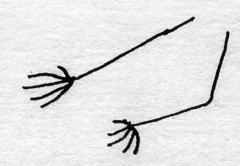

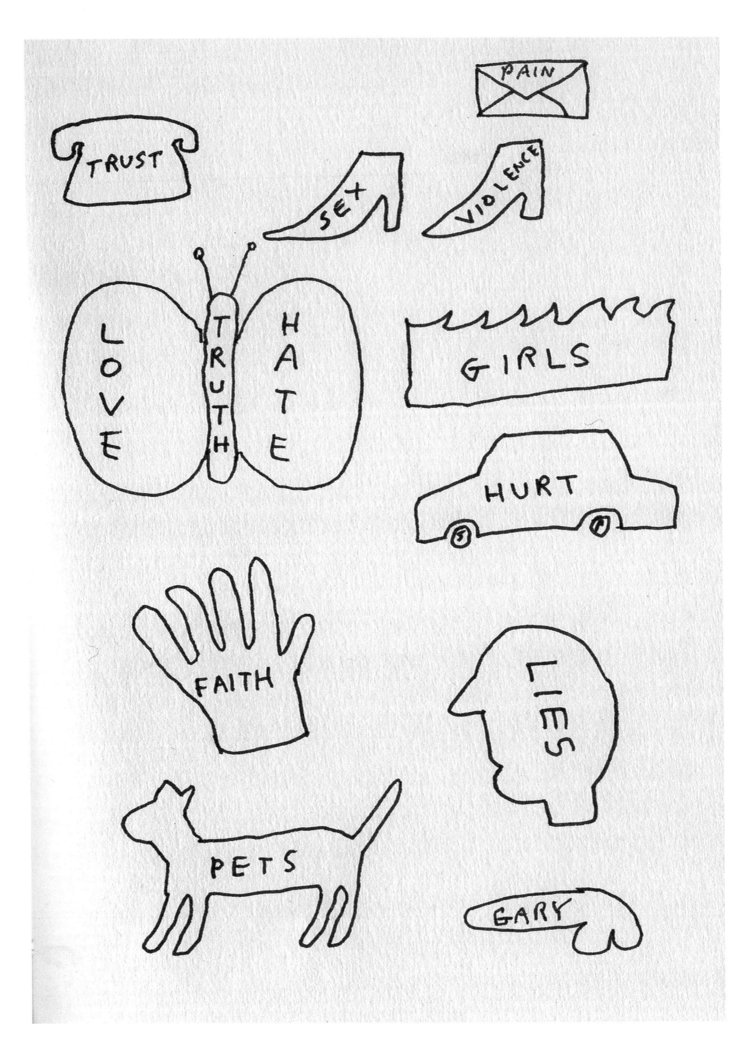

FANNY

BUM

KNOB

PUT ON
YOUR
PLIMSOLES
AND WE
WILL
WRESTLE

RIVER OF BLOOD

AFLOAT ON THE RIVER OF BLOOD:

CATAMARAN
FISHING BOAT
LIFE-BOAT
GONDOLA
CANOE
RAFT
OUTRIGGER
PUNT
DINGHY
MOTOR-BOAT
FERRY
HOVERCRAFT
SCHOONER
SLOOP
CUTTER
SKIFF
BARGE
CLIPPER
DREADNOUGHT
CRUISER
BATTLE-CRUISER
FRIGATE
GUNBOAT
AIRCRAFT CARRIER
DESTROYER
TORPEDO BOAT
TROOP SHIP
HOSPITAL SHIP
FIRESHIP

SLAVE SHIP
PADDLE-STEAMER
TUG
WHALER
TANKER
GALLEON
JUNK
DHOW
SAMPAN
LONG-BOAT
LAUNCH
DUCKS
SWANS
INSECTS
YACHT
LEAVES
DRIFTWOOD

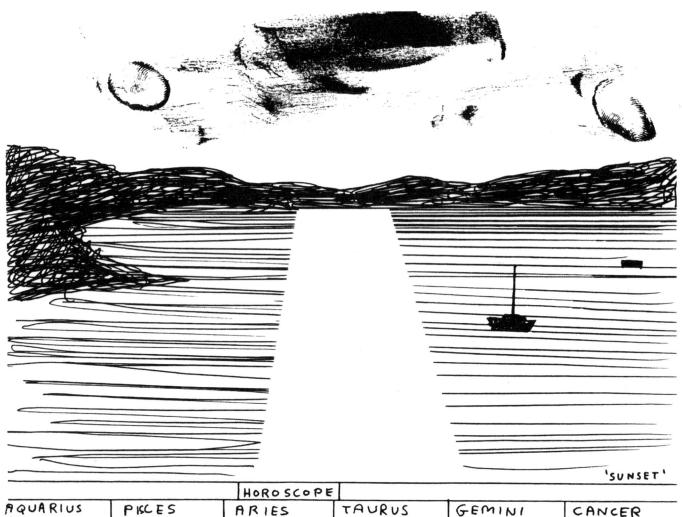

'SUNSET'

HOROSCOPE					
AQUARIUS	PISCES	ARIES	TAURUS	GEMINI	CANCER
YOU WILL ALMOST CERTAINLY WIN THE LOTTERY	YOU SHOULD GET DIVORCED	YOUR HOUSE WILL BURN DOWN		STAY OFF THE ROAD	THIS WEEK YOU WILL BECOME GRAVELY ILL
LEO	VIRGO	LIBRA	SCORPIO	SAGITTARIUS	CAPRICORN
STAY INDOORS	YOU ARE VERY TALL	YOU ARE A CRIMINAL AND YOU WILL GO TO JAIL	YOU WILL DIE NEXT WEEK	YOU WILL PROBABLY DIE THIS WEEK	YOU ARE AN ALCOHOLIC AND YOU WILL DIE THIS WEEK

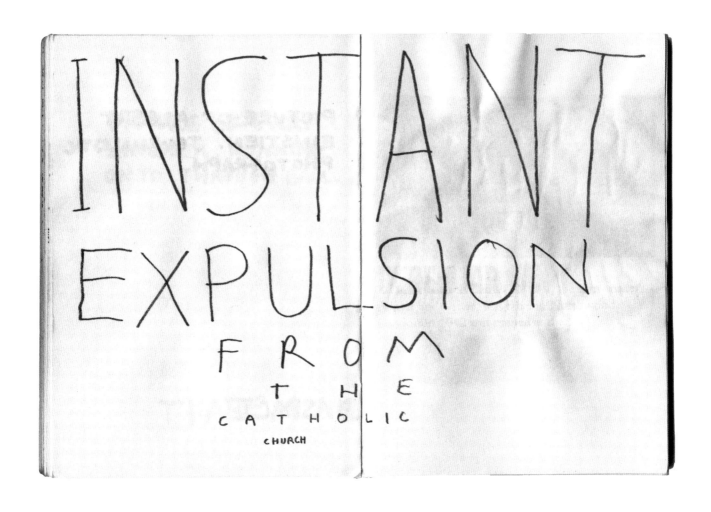

INSTANT
EXPULSION
FROM
THE
CATHOLIC
CHURCH

THEY PLACED A 'STUCK ON YOU' GARFIELD ON THEIR FRONT WINDSCREEN. THE 'STUCK ON YOU' GARFIELD WAS SO BIG THAT IT TOOK UP THE WHOLE WINDSCREEN SO THEY COULDN'T SEE OUT AND CRASHED THE CAR.

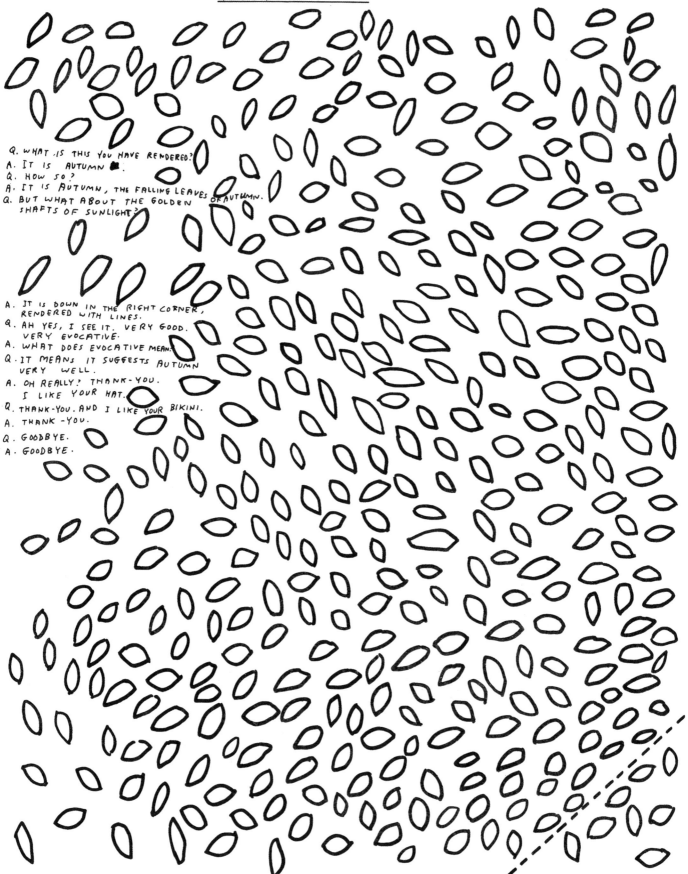

Q. WHAT IS THIS YOU HAVE RENDERED?
A. IT IS AUTUMN ●.
Q. HOW SO?
A. IT IS AUTUMN, THE FALLING LEAVES OF AUTUMN.
Q. BUT WHAT ABOUT THE GOLDEN
   SHAFTS OF SUNLIGHT?

A. IT IS DOWN IN THE RIGHT CORNER,
   RENDERED WITH LINES.
Q. AH YES, I SEE IT. VERY GOOD.
   VERY EVOCATIVE.
A. WHAT DOES EVOCATIVE MEAN?
Q. IT MEANS IT SUGGESTS AUTUMN
   VERY WELL.
A. OH REALLY? THANK-YOU.
   I LIKE YOUR HAT.
Q. THANK-YOU. AND I LIKE YOUR BIKINI.
A. THANK-YOU.
Q. GOODBYE.
A. GOODBYE.

140

BIOG.

AGE 0. — BORN ALREADY WITH HAIR AND TEETH
AGE 1. — GROWS THICK BUSHY BEARD AND STARTS TO USE FOUL LANGUAGE
2. — STARTS READING NOVELS BUT ONLY CRAP — CARL HIASSEN, ETC
3. — CAN PLAY THE SAXOPHONE ADMIRABLY AND BECOMES BRITISH 'CONNECT 4' CHAMPION
4. — LEARNS TO WALK. ▬▬ ▬▬
5. — TAKES A JOB AS A WINDOW CLEANER TO SUBSIDISE PRIVATE SCHOOLING
6. — FAILS CYCLING PROFICIENCY TEST
7. — LEARNS TO PLAY BADMINTON
8. — GIVES UP BADMINTON. TAKES UP WRESTLING
9. — GIVES UP WRESTLING.
10. — GAINS FIRST CLASS HONOURS DEGREE IN ARCHAEOLOGY FROM CAMBRIDGE UNIVERSITY
11. — FAILS TO FIND A JOB
12. — BECOMES MENTALLY ILL
13. — DIES

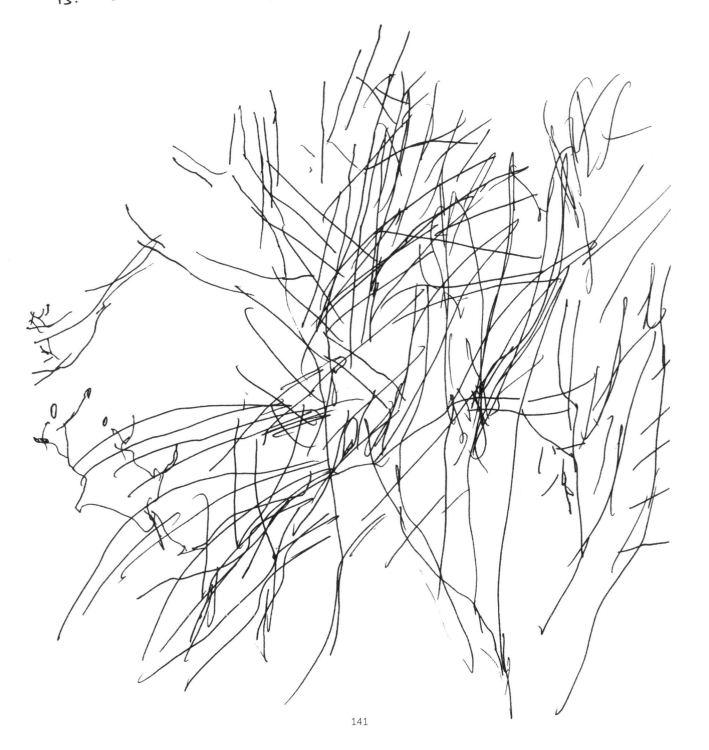

WE HAD SOME WONDERFUL TIMES TOGETHER

BUT THEN A FEW BAD THINGS HAPPENED

AND THINGS WERE GOOD AGAIN THE BEST THEY HAD EVER BEEN

BUT EVENTUALLY WE FORGOT ABOUT IT AND IT WAS OK AGAIN

THEN THERE WERE SOME PROBLEMS

BUT THEY WERE NOT SERIOUS

AND EVERYTHING WAS FINE AFTER THAT AND YOU STARTED TO PAINT

AND YOU BECAME VERY SUCCESSFUL AND I WAS CONSUMED BY JEALOUSY

142

I WENT AROUND ~~ME~~ ~~MY~~ MY BOSS'S, ~~HOUSE~~ HOME
AND STABBED ~~HER~~ IN THE EYE WITH THE
PLASTIC PENCIL FROM MY PALM PILOT

SHE MADE A LUNGE AT ME ~~BUT~~ BUT ONLY
CAUGHT MY DISCMAN WITH THE FORK/SPOON
SHE HAPPENED TO BE HOLDING

THE DISCMAN WAS STILL ON AFTER
WITH THE EARPHONES UNPLUGGED ~~AND~~ ~~SET~~
WITH ONE SIDE STILL IN MY EAR

SHE KNOCKED THE VEGETABLE JUICE ON THE FLOOR
THAT SHE HAPPENED TO BE DRINKING
THEN I KICKED HER TWICE
AND I LOST MY JOB

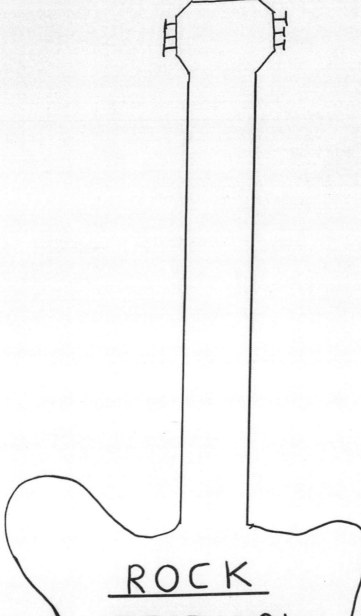

ROCK

FESTIVAL

THE SKY TURNS BLACK AND THE
HEAVENS OPEN. THERE IS TORRENTIAL
RAIN AND THUNDER AND LIGHT
-NING AND MANY ROCK STARS ARE
STRUCK BY LIGHTNING AND MEMBERS
OF THE AUDIENCE. THEN THERE IS
A HURRICANE AND ALL THE TENTS GET
BLOWN AWAY LEAVING EVERYONE SHIVERING
NAKED IN THE DARK. THEN THE RIVER
BURSTS ITS BANKS CAUSING A TERRIBLE
FLOOD AND THE STAGE COLLAPSES AND
EVERYTHING IS WASHED AWAY. THEN
THERE IS AND EARTHQUAKE AND THE
EARTH OPENS UP AND SWALLOWS
BIG TRUCKS AND PEOPLE AND AMPLIFIERS.
THEN THERE IS MORE THUNDER
AND LIGHTNING.

TODAY'S MENU

STARTERS	MAIN DISHES	DESSERT	DRINKS
SMALL BEASTS	LARGE BEASTS	CAKE	BLOOD

FLUFF AND WEEDS

SPECIAL SELECTION
100 %

MADE FROM OLD
SLEEPING BAGS
THAT TRAMPS HAVE DIED IN

Really stinks

YES!

I AM ASLEEP
MUM.

LOVE

KELLIG
xxx

I LIVE BEYOND THE MARGINS OF

SOCIETY.

I AM NOT ALLOWED TO ▓▓ JOIN

SOCIETY BECAUSE ▓▓▓▓▓▓▓▓▓▓

▓▓▓ ▓▓▓ ▓▓ ▓▓▓▓ ▓▓▓▓▓ ▓▓

I AM UNABLE TO GRASP THE

NUANCES OF HUMAN INTERACTION

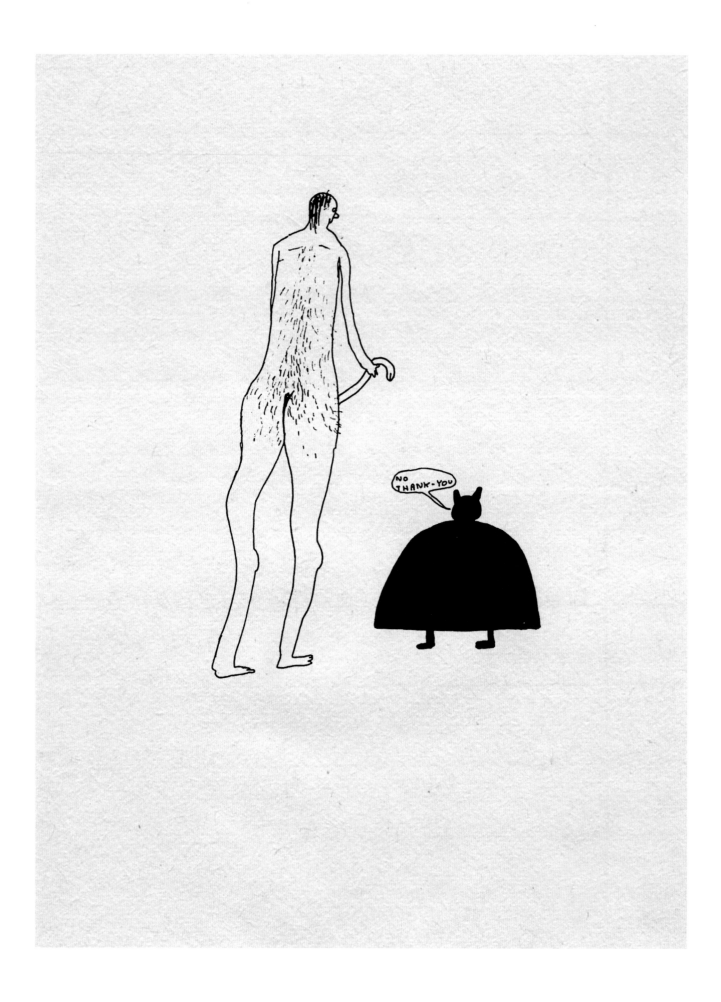

attatchements

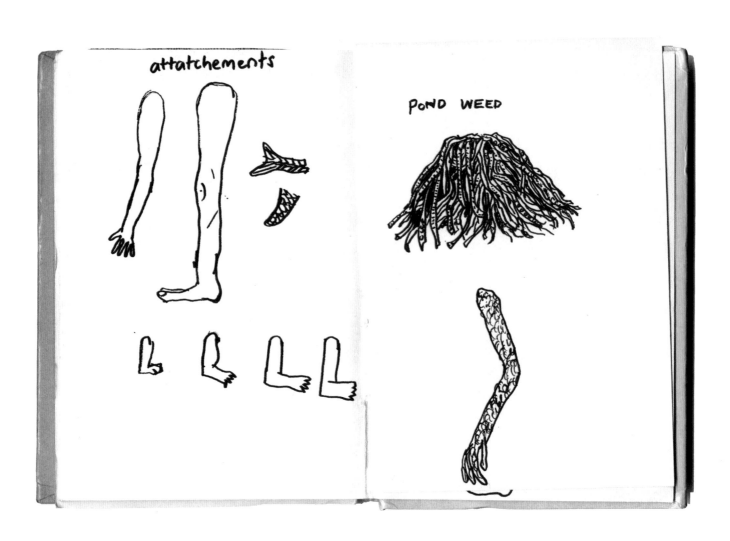

POND WEED

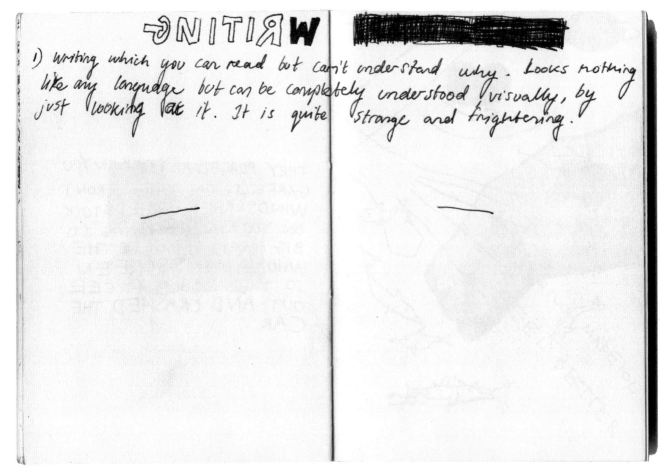

1) Writing which you can read but can't understand why. Looks nothing like any language but can be completely understood visually, by just looking at it. It is quite strange and frightening.

THE PAPER SCULPTURE

1. FOLD THE PAPER LENGTHWAYS WITH THE SHEEN OUTER
2. EARMARK THE WESTERNMOST CORNER OF THE STARBOARD HALF
3. TEAR THE REMAINING (PORT) HALF SLIGHTLY TO THE RIGHT AND CURVE THE THUS-CREATED RIDGE BETWEEN THE HEEL OF YOUR OTHER HAND (REVERSE IF YOU ARE EAST-HANDED) AND FOREFINGER
4. FOLD BOTH HEMISPHERES AGAIN QUICKLY AND THEN ONCE AGAIN AND THEN FLATTEN IT OUT
5. TURN THE PAPER OVER
6. REPEAT
7. YOU SHOULD NOW HAVE AN EVENLY DIVIDED PLANE OF TIGHT FOLDS POINTING UPWARDS. WHILST PRESSING ON THE NETHER-SIDE CORNER WITH THUMB AND/OR INDEX FINGER OF YOUR DOMINANT HAND, LIGHTLY BRUSH YOUR WEAKER INNER WRIST OVER THE PUCKERINGS IN A FORWARD MOTION UNTIL THEY ARE FLAT AGAIN
8. TAKE THE FAR CORNER OF THE PAPER UNDER YOUR LEFT OR RIGHT THUMB AND WITH YOUR OTHER THUMBNAIL, PARTLY SCORE A LINE FROM MIDDLE TO TOP, APPROXIMATELY TWO THIRDS FROM THE NEGATIVE EDGE.
9. GENTLY CURL THE UNINVOLVED PORTION UNTIL JUST BEFORE ITS NATURAL CREASING POINT, TAKING CARE NOT TO ACTUALLY GO OVER THE MARK
10. TAKE THE NORTH EDGE IN A SCISSOR-LIKE FASHION BETWEEN THE INDEX AND MIDDLE FINGER OF YOUR SUBORDINATE HAND, AND WITH YOUR OTHER ELBOW LOCATE AND FLATTEN THE APEX YOU HAVE PREVIOUSLY MADE.
11. MAKE A FIST ON YOUR LOWER SIDE AND SLOT THE MOST GAUNT EDGE INTO THE WIDEST TUCK BETWEEN YOUR FINGERS AND WITH THE BALL OF YOUR UN-USED FIST, DULL EACH EXTREMITY IN TURN UNTIL 'SPIT WILL NOT RUN OF IT'.
12. FOLD THE PAPER DIAGONALLY SEVERAL TIMES SO THAT THE CORNERS DON'T TOUCH, FLATTEN, REPEAT AND FLATTEN AGAIN
13. TAKING ADJACENT CORNERS BETWEEN THUMB AND SMALLEST FINGER, DRAW THE SHEET TOGETHER AND HOLD IT FOR 2-5 MINUTES
14. TURN THE SHEET OVER AND REPEAT
15. FIND A CYLINDER WITH A CIRCUMFERANCE NEAR AS DAMN IT EQUAL TO THE LONGEST EDGE OF THE PAPER (IF NO CYLINDER IS AVAILABLE YOU MAY USE ONE OF YOUR LIMBS)
16. FASTEN THE SHEET AROUND THE CYLINDER/LIMB WITH A PIECE OF TAPE.
17. WRITE THE NAMES OF THINGS WHICH YOU LIKE ON THE PAPER
18. UNFASTEN
19. MAKE THE PAGE INTO WHAT YOU CONSIDER TO BE A NONAGON, WITH THE FLAPS POINTING DOWN
20. WITH YOUR RIGHT HAND MANIPULATE THE SHEET SLIGHTLY WITH A FLATTENED PALM UNTIL THE FACING SIDE LOOKS LIKE (WHAT YOU UNDERSTAND TO BE) A ROUGH TRAPEZOID FROM WHERE YOU ARE SITTING / STANDING
21. THEN MOVE YOUR OTHER HAND AROUND THE PIECE AND APPROXIMATE THE EXACT OPPOSITE ACTION (AGAIN WITH A FLATTENED PALM) WHICH YOU HAVE JUST UNDERTAKEN WITH YOUR RIGHT HAND UNTIL THE SHEET TAKES BACK (WHAT YOU REMEMBER AS) ITS FORMER SHAPE
22. UNFOLD.

TAKING CUES

THE PREVIOUS FOUR PAGES HAVE HAD SEVERAL CUES CONTAINED IN THEM TO STIMULATE THE READER INTO ACTION

WHAT DO YOU THINK ABOUT WHEN YOU'RE KNITTING ?

ADVERTISMENT FOR DENIM TROUSERS

THE GRAVESTONE WHEN THE IMAGE OF THE GRAVESTONE ~~WAS~~ FIRST PRINTED A GROSS ERROR WAS MADE. WE DID NOT KNOW AT THE TIME BUT APPARENTLY THE IMAGE USED WAS TAKEN FROM AN 'ETCHING' (WHATEVER THAT IS) MADE BY A CRAZY FROM THE COLLEGE. IT DIDNT RESEMBLE ANYTHING AND WAS JUST AN INSULT TO THE FAMILY

HE WAS SAYING THAT HE HAD
LAMBS AVAILABLE FOR SLAUGHTER

I SAID WAS IT POSSIBLE TO
BUY SOME LAMBS ALREADY SLAUGHTERED?

AS I DID NOT WANT TO DO
THE SLAUGHTERING MYSELF

HE SAID IT WAS NOT POSSIBLE
FOR HIM TO DO THE SLAUGHTERING
AS ONE OF HIS ARMS WAS PART MISSING
AND THE OTHER ONE WAS BAD

AND ~~THE~~ BESIDES HE SAID HE
FELT THE SAME AS ME ABOUT
SLAUGHTERING

UNSLAUGHTERED
HE SAID HE WOULD SELL ME ~~SLAUGHTERED~~
LAMBS AND I COULD GET ANOTHER
MAN TO DO THE SLAUGHTERING

BUT THAT WAS IT HE SAID
THAT WAS HIS FINAL OFFER

WORDS TRANSLATED
FROM THE FOREIGN:

"WHEN YOU ARE BEHEADED CAN I HAVE YOUR HEAD?"

"IS IT YOU THAT IS GETTING MARRIED OR IS IT THE OTHER MAN?"

"HOW DID YOU FOLD YOUR PARACHUTE SO NEAT

"WHAT IS IT WITH YOU AND YOUR WAYS?"

"DON'T YOU UNDERSTANT ~~WHE~~ WHAT IS GOING ON?

"CAN YOU PLEASE PASS THE SOLVENT"

"MY FATHER IS YOUR BROTHER IS THAT MEANS WE AREN'T SISTERS AS YOU SAY WE ARE"

"TAKE THIS PRECIOUS METAL AND MAKE IT INTO A RING"

"I'M FED UP WITH LISTENING TO YOUR GROANING"

"IF YOU READ WITH THAT LOOK ON YOUR FACE I'M NOT GOING TO LISTEN"

"I WAS ILL AND STILL AM NOT ENTIRELY WELL"

OUR TEACHER

SHE NEVER LET US WASTE ▬▬▬▬

A SINGLE PIECE OF PAPER

YOUR HEART LEAPS...........BECAUSE YOU ARE ❋ UNREALISTI

YOU SMILE.........................BECAUSE YOU ARE STUPID

YOU LAUGH AND DANCE..........WE LAUGH AT YOU

CAR ALARMS SOUND SARCASTIC
TO YOU

THE UGLIEST
OF THE
DEFORMED

YOU ARE SO UGLY
NO ONE WILL GIVE
YOU A HAIRCUT

THESE ARE

YOUR THINGS

CHANGES OF DIRECTION

I DON'T WANT TO WRITE
NOVELS ANYMORE,
I WANT TO CUT HAIR

I DON'T WANT TO BE A DOCTOR ANYMORE,
I WANT TO BE A BOXER

I DON'T WANT TO BE A DRIVING INSTRUCTOR ANYMORE,
I WANT TO BE A BUTCHER

WE DON'T WORSHIP GOD
NOW WE
WORSHIP ELECTRICITY

HOW STRUCTURES ARE GOT TO BY WORD-MAPS
WHEN WE ARE STRANGELY AWAKE;

HALF OF THE TIME THEY ARE NOT REALLY USEFUL AT A
MOST OF THE TIME THEY ILLUSTRATE US AS FOOLS
HAPHAZARD CHANCE IS REALLY THE ROOT OF IT

MODERN NATURE

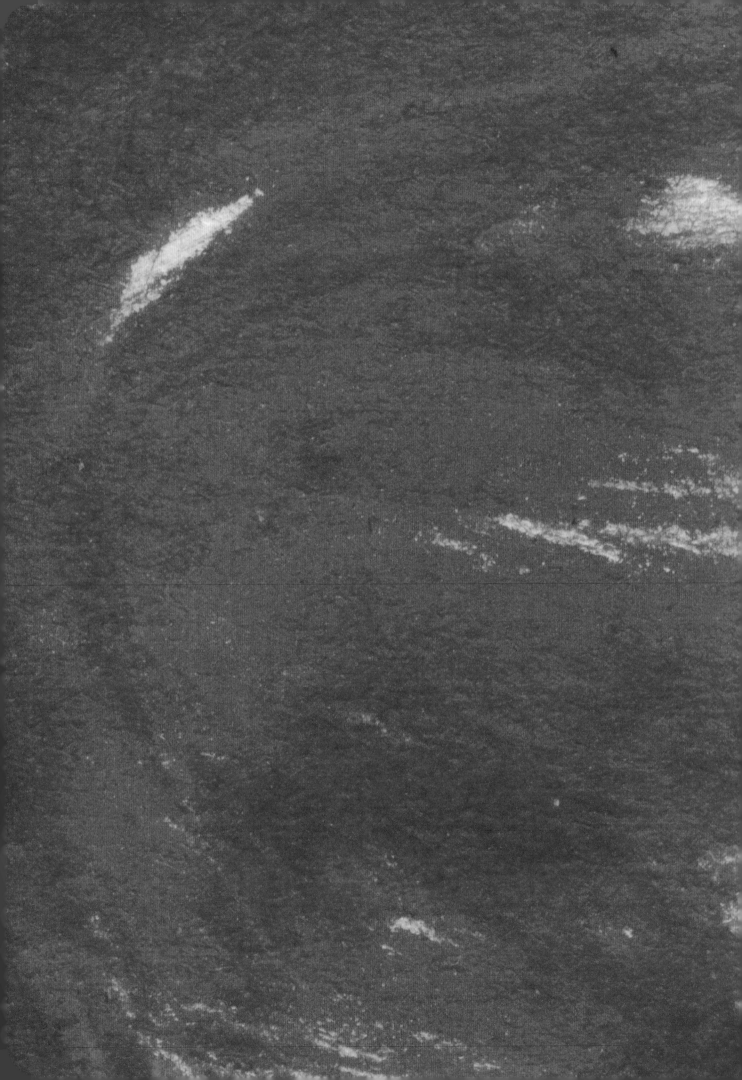

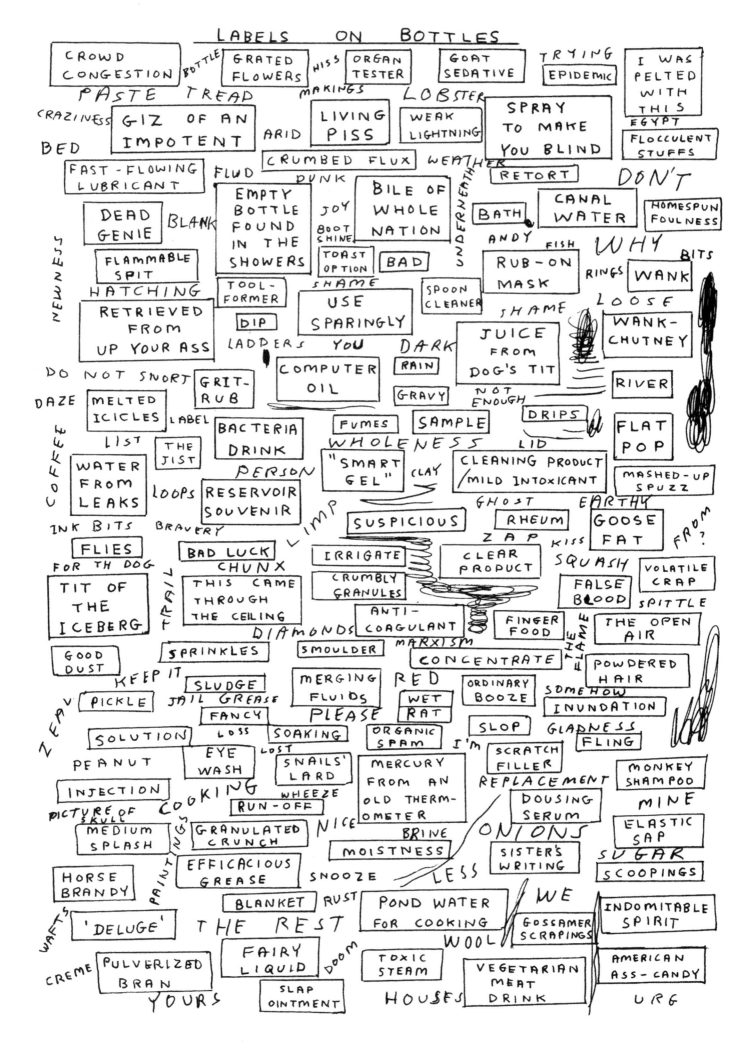

DRAINO
PLUNGER
RCA CABLES
PEACHES
BATH TUB SCRUB
BRUSH

"I want all children who graduate from California schools to know how to read, write and speak English."

Paul Zee
City Councilmember/Businessman
(626) 403-7777

To Banararama,
You are the best group in the world! Could I join your fan club. Could your please send things of Banararama because I ~~am~~ collect all sorts of things with your three in it. Do you think I could have some of your clothes because I think they are fab! Also could you send some hairstyle copies for ME!
THANKS   Age 13
love Diane.S.
Please could make

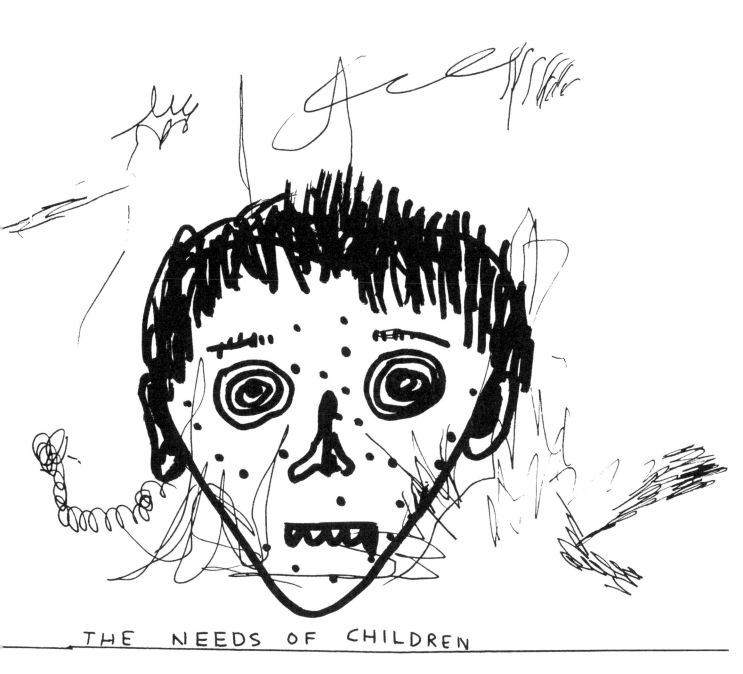

THE NEEDS OF CHILDREN

SUGAR
PETS

STOP
THE LAP
DANCE I
WANT TO
GO HOME

Internal telephone numbers in the hotel

PLACE .... DIAL
----
reception .... 111 or 110
breakfast room 113

ROOM No. .... DIAL
----
101 101
102 102
103 103
104 104
105 105
106 106

201 201
202 202
203 203
204 204
205 205
206 206
207 207

301 301
302 302
303 303
304 304
305 305
306 306
307 307

401 401
402 402

You can dial any international or local call directly from your room, dial 0 and then the number. For calling from your room to another, please dial its number.

FACT FILE

1. TOMATOES DON'T GROW IN WINTER
2. HIGHEST MOUNTAIN IS IN WALES
3. BALOONS INVENTED IN 1783
4. ICONOCGRAPHICAL EMBLEM OF BROKEN CUP IS THAT OF ABBOT BENEDICT
5. CAPITAL OF TONGA IS NUKU'ALOFA

FOREWORD TO FACT FILE

HAVE YOU EVER TRIED TO FIND THE ANSWER TO WHAT YOU THOUGHT WAS A RELATIVELY SIMPLE QUESTION? HAVE YOU SEARCHED HIGH AND LOW AND FINALLY GIVEN UP IN COMPLETE EXASPERTION? THE 'FACT FILE' IS THE LIST YOU NEED, WITH SEVERAL DIFFICULT-TO-REMEMBER AND HARD-TO-FIND FACTS. HERE YOU WILL FIND THE ANSWERS TO SUCH DIVERSE ENQUIRIES AS 'DO TOMATOES GROW IN WINTER?' AND 'WHEN WERE BALOONS INVENTED?'. LIKE ITS NUMERICAL COMPANION, 'READY REFERENCE', 'FACT FILE' PROVIDES AN EASY-TO-USE QUICK REFERENCE POINT TO A BROAD MISCELLANY OF INFORMATION THAT COULD ONLY BE OTHERWISE OBTAINED AFTER CONSULTING A WIDE VARIETY OF SOURCES, AND AS SUCH WILL APPEAL TO EVERYONE FROM TRIVIA BUFFS AND QUIZ COMPILERS TO STUDENTS AND JOURNALISTS.

VICTIM OF NO PREJUDICE

I HATE YOU + WANT TO DIE

MIDDLE CLASS BOY OF MONIED PARENTS WEARS MAKE-UP + MUM'S DRESSES.

WHY IS HE SO ANGRY?

HE IS WASTING THE HANDSOME START HE HAD IN LIFE. . . . .

TWAT

THE BASIC PRINCIPLES OF TYPOGRAPHY

SPACING
EMPHASIS
HEADLINES
NUMERALS

THESE

NUTS

PRETENTIOUS

TOO FANCY

UPPER CASE

THESE OF COURSE MAY NOT BE PRESENT

CHAPTER ONE

FANTASY

(RED)

BLANK
BLANK
INSERT QUOTATION MARKS
BLANK
LIST
BLANK
~~CLOSED~~ COMMENTS
BLANK

NOW

COMPUTERS HAVE CHANGED EVERYTHING
AND THE WAY ~~THAT~~ WE GO ABOUT IT

TEN EUROS

I   SPIT ON YOUR TEN EUROS
IT IS AN INSULT

I TAKE YOUR TEN EUROS
AND I SPEND IT ON CRAP
THINGS THAT I DON'T NEED
I   SPEND IT ON DOG FOOD
I   AM NOT A RICH MAN
I   AM A POOR MAN
I LIVE IN A TENT
AND STILL I LAUGH AT YOUR TEN EUROS
SENT TO ME THROUGH THE POST
THIS DAY
THIS FRIDAY THE FIFTEENTH OF
OCTOBER
IN AN ENVELOPE
~~————————~~

I   PUT THE ENVELOPE ON THE FIRE
AND I SPEND YOUR TEN EUROS
ON CRAP
HA !

WILL YOU JOIN ME

IN MAKING THIS SCULPTURE OF YODA (THE WEE MAN FROM STAR WARS)?

WILL YOU JOIN ME

IN CASTING THESE BEAUTIFUL GEMS AMOUNG THE SWINE?

WILL YOU JOIN ME

IN LUNCHEON AT MY FLAT NEXT WEEK? I AM FINDING IT INCREASINGLY DIFFICULT TO MAKE FREINDS BECAUSE OF MY DREADFUL ACNE.

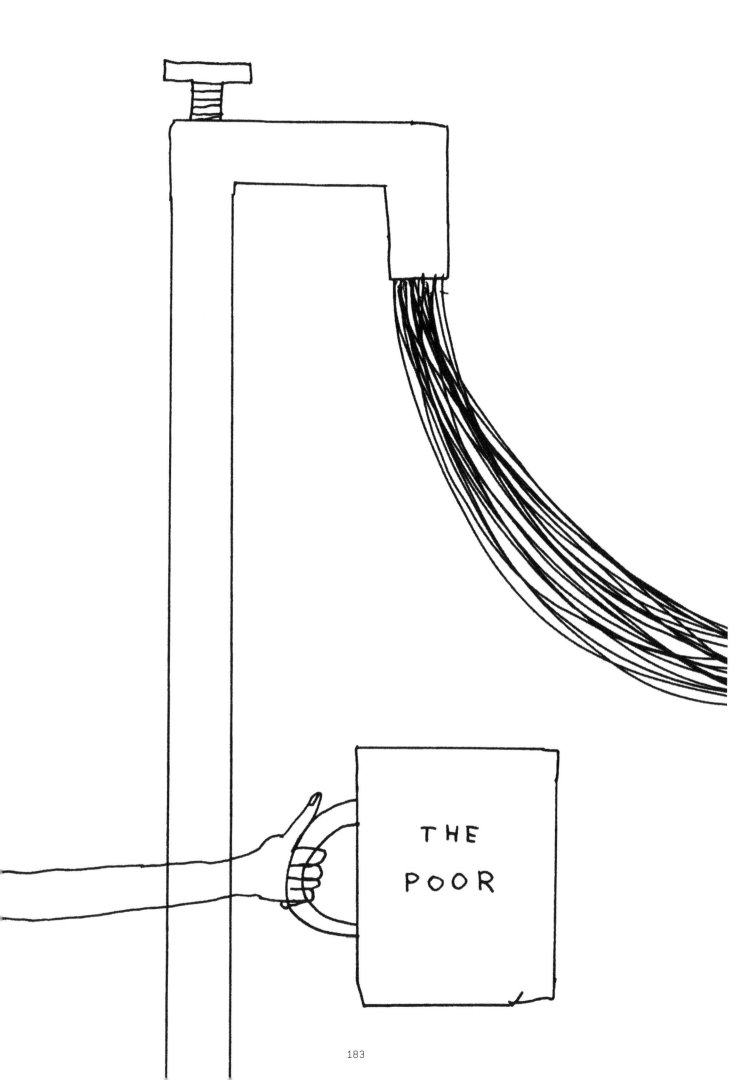

THE

POOR

WHAT ~~SHOULD~~ SHOULD HAVE HELD YOUR ATTENTION	WHAT DID HOLD YOUR ATTENTION
AMAZING FIREWORK DISPLAY LASTING FOR HOURS. MUST HAVE COST THOUSANDS. THE MOST AWESOME DISPLAY EVER HELD.	CLOTHES PEG HANGING FROM A PIECE OF STRING.
YOUR WIFE GIVING BIRTH	MIDWIFE'S WART
SURFACING OF ANCIENT GALLEON AFTER BEING LIFTED FROM OCEAN BED.	MAYFLY DROWNIG IN POOL OF SPIT
THE MOVIE 'CITIZEN KANE'	OLD CARPET
HER DANCING	HER GRAN WATCHING
LIONS FIGHTING	TOENAILS
THE GHOST OF YOUR LONG-DEAD FATHER	A LEAF MOVING SLIGHTLY IN THE WIN
EXAM RESULT	ENVELOPE IT CAME IN
COMET	CIGARETTE
FIRE ALARM	T.V.
ENORMOUS SATELLITE DISH	SUNGLASSES
ROSE GARDEN	REMAINS OF CHINESE MEAL; TIN FOI CARTONS, UNEATEN PRAWN CRACKERS, E
~~██~~ LAUNCH OF SPACE ROCKET	RULER

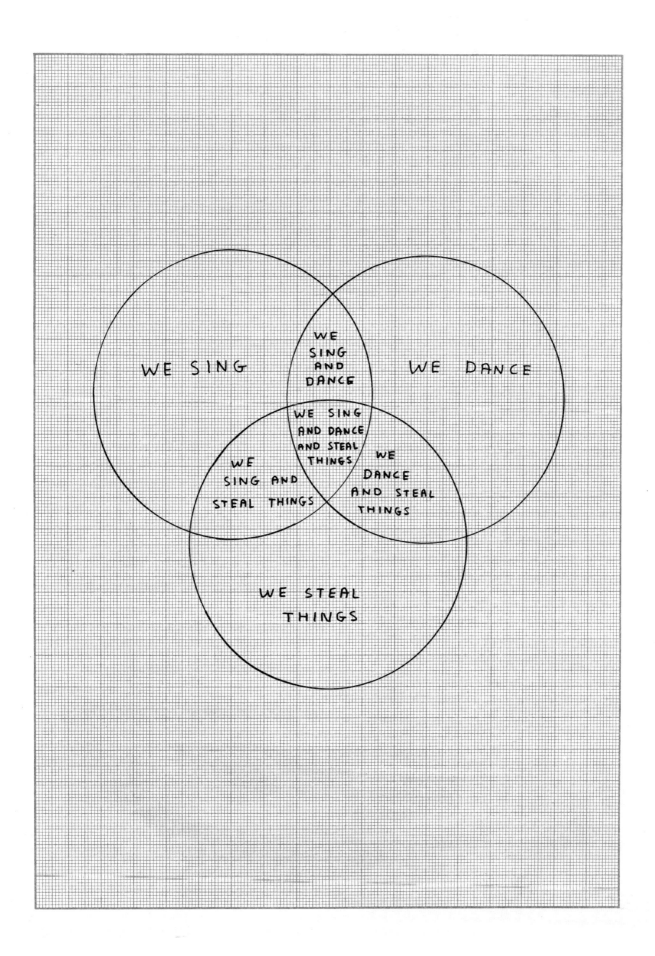

GLUTTONY
GREED
SLOTH
ENVY
WRATH
PRIDE
LUST
CAR CRASH

(MAKE YOUR CHOICE AND
THEN CHOOSE ONE OTHER
IN CASE YOUR FIRST
CHOICE IS UNAVAILABLE.)

DRUGS MAKE US STRONGER

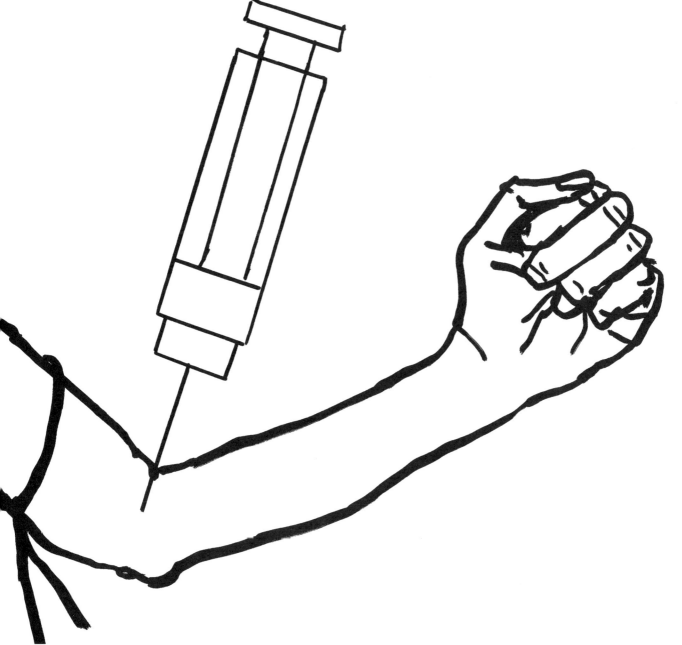

I DID EVERYTHING ON THE LIST
JUST AS YOU ASKED ME
I BOUGHT ALL THE ITEMS
I MADE ALL THE PHONE CALLS
I DELIVERED ALL THE PARCELS
I DID THE TIDYING
I CLEANED THE THINGS
I FED THE ANIMALS
I BRUSHED MY HAIR
WHAT DO I DO NOW ?

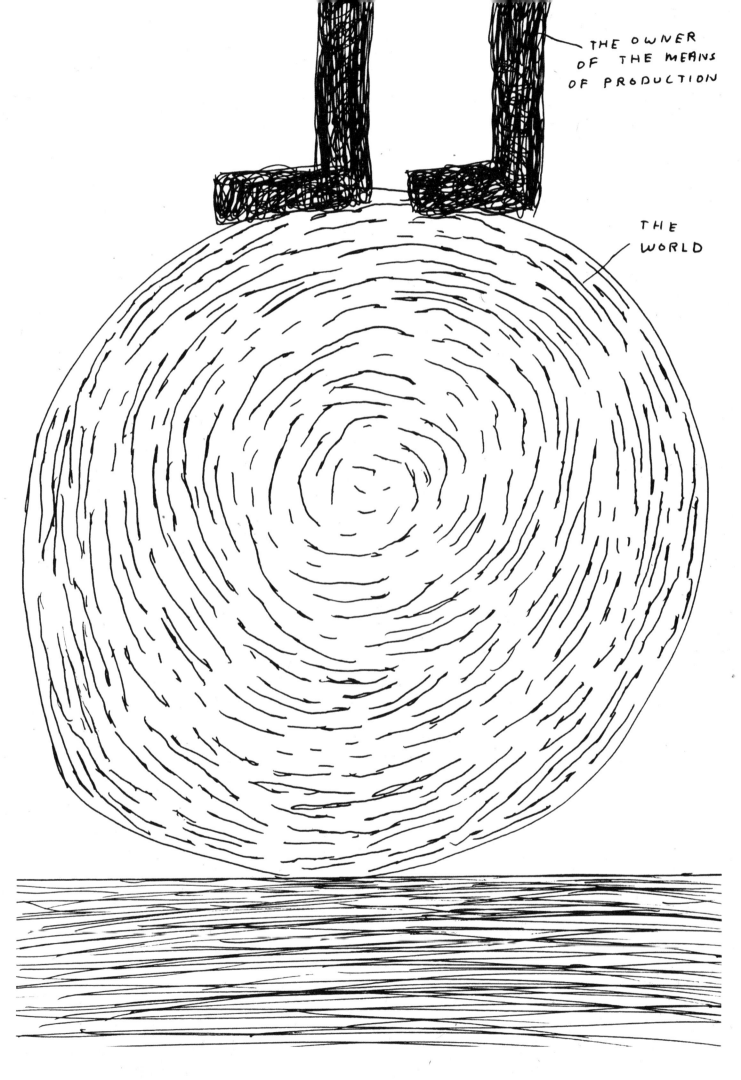

THE OWNER
OF THE MEANS
OF PRODUCTION

THE
WORLD

NO TOURNAMENT

FIRST LOUSE :
 LET'S HAVE A TOURNAMENT
SECOND LOUSE :
 WHAT KIND OF TOURNAMENT?
FIRST LOUSE :
 A TOURNAMENT TO SEE
WHO IS THE BETTER
BETWEEN US
 SECOND LOUSE :
 TO WHAT END ?
 FIRST LOUSE :
 TO ESTABLISH DOMINANCE
SECOND LOUSE :
 BUT WE ARE LICE AND
HAVE NO HEIRARCHY.
WE DO NOT EVEN HAVE
NAMES.

SLOW

TODAY, THIS AFTERNOON IS GOING
SO DAMN SLOWLY

 SLOW AS A BEARD

GROWING SILENTLY ON YOUR

FACE

SLOW AS A CHILD WITH A

DAMAGED BRAIN

IT IS SO

SLOW IT MAKES ME ANGRY

THIS KIND OF SLOW

ADDLES THE MIND AND MAKES
KILLERS AND PSYCHOPATHS OF US ALL

I SAID I WOULD
MAKE HER SOME-
THING NICE FOR
WHEN SHE GOT
BACK FROM YOGA
- I WAS LYING

<u>IT IS 4 PM . I AM HUNGOVER</u>
<u>+ HAVE THE FEAR ;</u>

☹ PINDROP SHATTERS EARTH'S
   SURFACE.

☹ I DO TIGHTROPE WALK
   ONE MILE UP , NO NET.

😠 I AWAKE DAMP FROM
   CHEESEWIRE CASTRATION ~~NIGHTMARE~~
   TO FIND BEDSHEETS SOAKED
   WITH BLOOD, ETC.

🙂 KERI COMES HOME SHIT-FACED
   AND DOESN'T CLOSE FRONT DOOR
   I AM ATTACKED BY PSYCHO
   ON MY WAY TO THE TOILET.

-: THUS :-

<u>I MUST INGEST CAKE</u>
<u>+ BAKED POTATO TO MAKE</u>
<u>ME WELL</u>

DESPITE OUR EFFORTS
THE Y's STILL PROLIFERATE

GETTING INTO SHRIGLEY

I STAND ALONE

BECAUSE MY WORDS ARE UNACCEPTABLE TO OTHERS

THE ESSENCE (OR 'JIST')

I WILL DO MY BEST TO EXPLAIN IT

IT IS NOT IN THE THINKING OF NEW THINGS TO DO

IT IS IN THE COUNTING OF THINGS THAT YOU HAVE ALREADY DONE

AND IT IS NOT IN THE THINGS YOU STAPLE TOGETHER

IT IS IN YOUR DESIRE TO STAPLE

AND IT IS NOT IN THE SPEAKING ON THE TELEPHONE

IT IS IN HOW LOUD YOU ARE SPEAKING

AND IT IS NOT IN THE CABLE T.V.

IT IS IN THE CABLES THEMSELVES THROUGH WHICH THEY SEND THE CRAP INTO OUR HOMES

AND IT IS NOT IN THE SMILING

IT IS IN THE TEETH BENEATH THE SMILE AND ALSO THE TONGUE

AND IT IS NOT IN THE BAYING FOR BLOOD

IT IS IN THE ACTUAL BAYING, THE QUALITY OF THE BAYING

AND IT IS NOT IN THE PLASTIC BOTTLE

IT IS IN THE COLOUR OF THE LID OF THE PLASTIC BOTTLE

AND IT IS NOT IN HER ACTIONS OR WORDS

IT IS IN HOW MUCH HER ACTIONS OR WORDS ANNOY YOU

AND IT IS NOT IN YOUR THRESHING MACHINE

IT IS IN HOW MUCH YOUR WORKERS ARE AFRAID OF THE THRESHING MACHINE

AND IT IS NOT IN THE CHOCOLATE FACTORY

IT IS IN THE VERY FACT THAT THERE IS A CHOCOLATE FACTORY

AND IT IS NOT IN 'THE CHAIR'

IT IS IN THE LIST THAT DOES EXIST SOMEWHERE OF ALL THE PEOPLE WHO HAVE SAT IN 'THE CHAIR'

AND IT IS NOT IN PINEAPPLE CHUNKS

IT IS IN PINEAPPLE RINGS

AND IT IS NOT IN ROCKET FUEL

IT IS IN THE DRINKING OF ROCKET FUEL

AND IT IS NOT IN JOKES

IT IS IN THE NEED FOR JOKES

AND IT IS NOT IN TIME, EXACTLY

IT IS IN THE SAND IN THE HOUR GLASS

AND IT IS NOT IN BOOKS

IT IS IN THE SOBER ATMOSPHERE OF THE LIBRARY

AND IT IS NOT IN BANGING ON THE BIG BASS DRUM

IT IS IN THE INAUDIBLE SWISHING OF THE CONDUCTOR'S BATON

AND IT IS NOT IN THE DEVIL YOU KNOW

IT IS IN THE DEVIL YOU DON'T KNOW

AND IT IS NOT IN THE PIE FILLING

IT IS IN THE PASTRY

AND IT IS NOT IN THE RUBBISH

IT IS IN WHERE YOU PUT THE RUBBISH

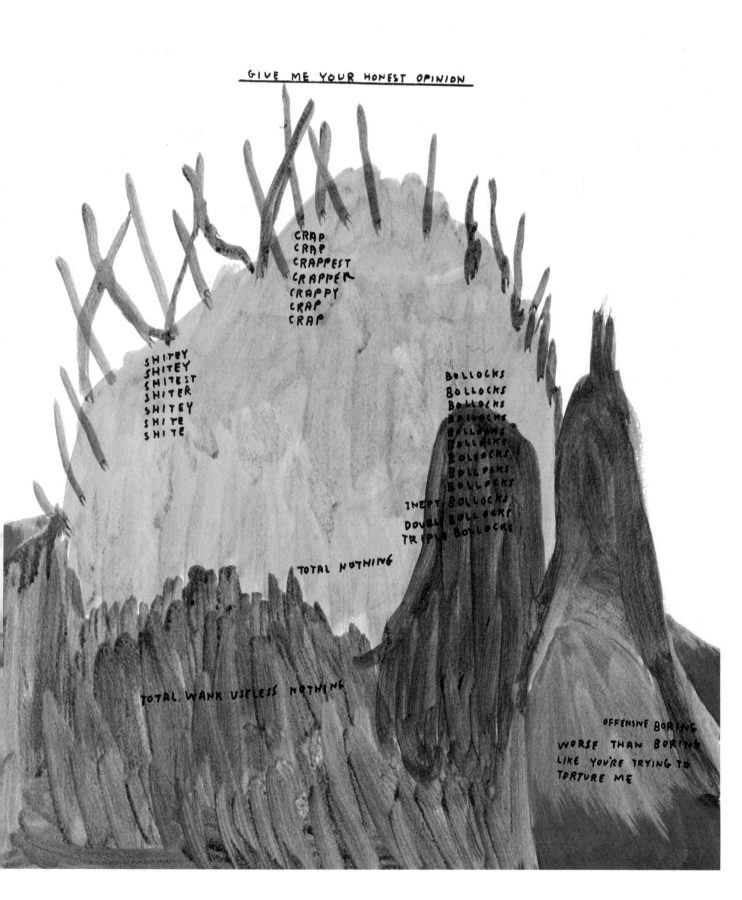

ONCE I SAW SOME TEXT WRITTEN-
DOWN ON A PAGE. IT WASN'T
PRINTED BUT HAND-WRITTEN IN
BLACK (INK, I PRESUME) PROBABLY
WITH SOME FAIRLY SOPHISTICATED
WRITING TOOL (DEFINITELY NOT A
STICK, POSSIBLY A BALL-POINT PEN).
SINCE I CANNOT READ I DO NOT
KNOW WHAT ██████ IT SAID. IT MIGHT
HAVE BEEN WRITTEN IN A FORIEGN
LANGUAGE OR HAVE BEEN OBSCENE.
IT MIGHT HAVE BEEN IMPORTANT
OR IT MIGHT HAVE BEEN VERY
TRIVIAL ; I JUST DON'T KNOW.
I STILL WONDER ABOUT IT SOMETIMES
WHEN I AM WATCHING MY GIRLFRIEND
READ THE NEWSPAPER.

DEPTH

MAP OR MODEL OR DESIGN OR SOMETHING
OF SOMETHING RENDERED BY SOMEONE
OR A COMPUTER OR BOTH TO HELP
SOMEBODY OR GROUP OF SOMEBODIES
TO BETTER SEE OR UNDERSTAND OR
SOMETHING SOMETHING OR OTHER
SOMETHING IN MORE OR LESS DETAIL
OR SOMETHING OR FROM A DISTANCE
PERHAPS

INBETWEEN BOLD

STRIPES IS WHERE I BELONG

I AM HAPPY NOWHERE ELSE

NOT ONTOP OF NOR BELOW

NOR TO THE SIDES BUT

INBETWEEN BOLD

STRIPES IS WHERE I BELONG

I AM HAPPY NOWHERE ELSE

NOT ONTOP OF NOR BELOW

NOR TO THE SIDES BUT

FIRST IMPRESSIONS

I COULD TELL THAT
YOU WERE NERVOUS
BECAUSE YOU WERE
SHAKING LIKE A STICK
I COULD TELL THAT
YOU WERE ANGRY
BECAUSE YOU WERE
GROWLING LIKE A DOG
I COULD TELL THAT
YOU WERE HOT BECAUSE
YOU WERE SWEATING
LIKE A HORSE
I COULD TELL THAT
YOU WERE MENTAL
BECAUSE YOU WERE
WEARING A STRAIGHT-
JACKET AND YOU WERE
CHAINED TO THE WALL.
APART FROM THAT YOU
WERE A MYSTERY.

AN EXPLANATION OF SORTS

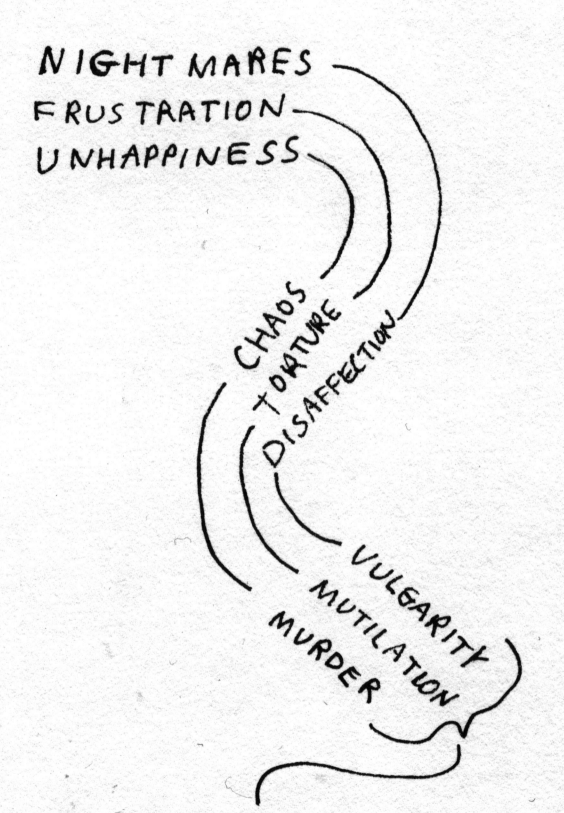

NIGHTMARES
FRUSTRATION
UNHAPPINESS

CHAOS
TORTURE
DISAFFECTION

VULGARITY
MUTILATION
MURDER

AN ULTIMATE PEACE

I STARTED WRITING A LIST

1. THOSE WHO SUFFER TERRIBLY
1.A. THOSE WHO DON'T SUFFER AT ALL
1.B. THOSE WHO SUFFER MODERATELY
2. THOSE WHO WOULD SELL EVERYTHING THEY OWNED TO TURN BACK THE CLOCK
2.A. THOSE WHO WOULD NOT GIVE A PIECE OF CORN TO TURN BACK THE CLOCK
2.B. THOSE WHO HAVE NEVER THOUGHT ABOUT IT.
3. THOSE WHO WOULD THROW THE COMPUTER OUT OF THE WINDOW
3A. THOSE WHO WOULD NOT
3B. THOSE WHO WOULD THROW PARTS OF THE COMPUTER OUT OF THE WINDOW
4. THOSE WHO WOULD UP AND LEAVE JUST LIKE THAT
4.A. THOSE WHO WOULDN'T
4B. THOSE WHO MIGHT
5. THOSE WHO WOULD KILL
5A. THOSE WHO WOULD NOT
5B. THOSE WHO WOULDN'T KILL BUT WOULD GLADLY MAIM
6. THOSE WHO WOULD TOLERATE IT
6.A. THOSE WHO WOULD MAKE A FUSS
6.B. THOSE WHO WOULDN'T HAVE PUT THEMSELVES IN THAT POSITION IN THE FIRST PLACE.
7. THOSE WHO HAVE SPENT THEIR LIVES PRODUCTIVELY
7A. THOSE WHO HAVE WASTED THEIR LIVES
7.B. THOSE WHO REFUSE TO ANSWER THE QUESTION
8. THOSE WHO PAY FOR DOMESTIC HELP
8.A. THOSE WHO KEEP SLAVES
8.B. THOSE WHOSE HOUSES ARE DIRTY
9. THOSE WHOSE CHARM IS MOST EVIDENT
9.A. THOSE WHOSE CHARM IS HIDDEN
9B. THE CHARMLESS
10. THOSE WHO THROW STICKS
10A. THOSE WHO CHASE STICKS
10B. THOSE WHO DON'T LIKE SPORT
11. THOSE WHO GET THE FEAR
11A. THE FEARLESS
11B. THOSE WHO GIVE OTHER PEOPLE THE FEAR

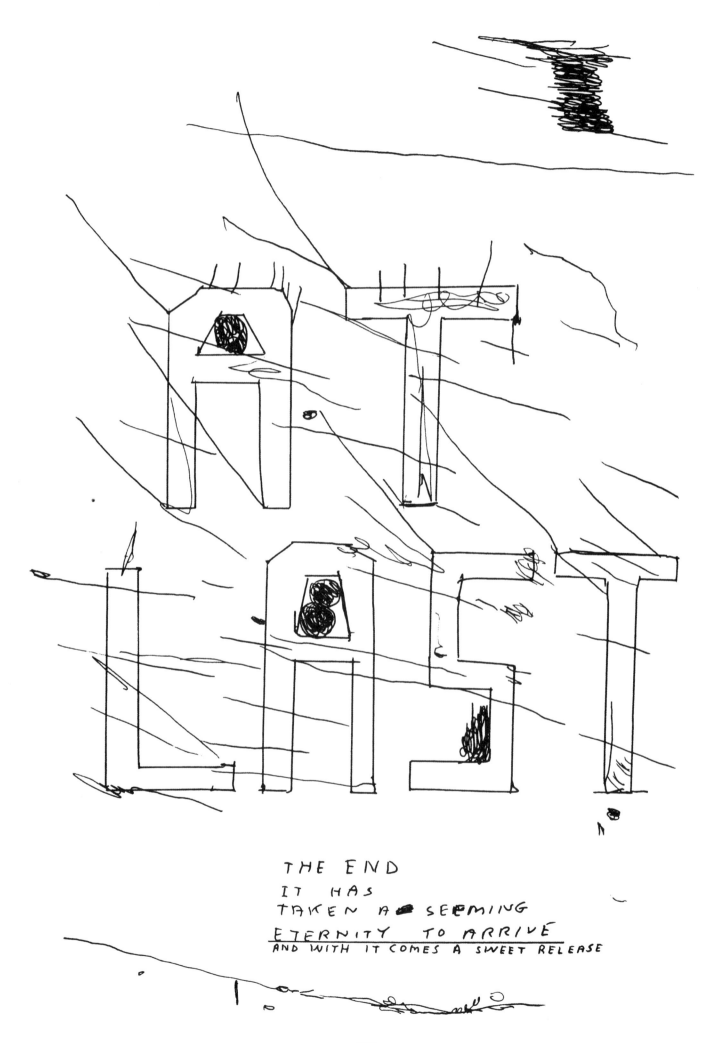

THE END
IT HAS
TAKEN A SEEMING
ETERNITY TO ARRIVE
AND WITH IT COMES A SWEET RELEASE

BOOKS BY
DAVID SH.

Black Rose, 1992

Black Rose, 1992

Armpit Press, 1994

(ENQUIRE WITHIN) Armpit Press, 1995

Armpit Press, 1996

Tramway, 1996

Bookworks, 1996

Galleri Nicolai Wallner, 1998

Little Cockroach Press, 1998

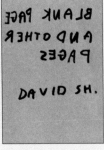

Modern Institute, 1998

Redstone Press, 1998

Armpit Press, 1998

Redstone Press, 1999

Pocketbooks, 2000

Galleri Nicolai Wallner, 2000

Redstone Press, 2001

Redstone Press, 2002

Kunsthaus, 2003

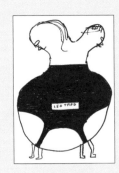

BQ, 2003

Redstone Press, 2003

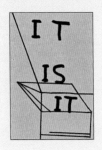

Nieves, 2004

Galleri Nicolai Wallner, 2004

Redstone Press, 2004

Redstone Press, 2004

LIST OF WORKS

1 (Endpaper) Sketchbook, 1995
5 Prepare Yourself, Sketchbook, 1994
6 'How I Fly', *Blank Page and Other Pages*, The Modern Institute, 1998

LIFE, OR, IS THAT IT?

15 'Light Source', Private Collection, courtesy Stephen Friedman Gallery, 1999
16 'I Attempts to Write', Private Collection, courtesy Stephen Friedman Gallery, 2002
17 'Everyone Loves a Turtle', Sketchbook, 1990
18 'Have a Wank', *Blocked Path*, Galleri Nicolai Wallner, Denmark, 2004
19 'Message to Everyone', *Insert*, for Parkett, 1998
20 'How Time Is Kept', Private Collection, courtesy Stephen Friedman Gallery, 1998
21 'The Little Red Nuts', Private Collection, courtesy Stephen Friedman Gallery, 2000
22 'Please Clean the Refrigerator', Private Collection, 2001
23 'Problem Child', *Centre Parting*, Little Cockroach Press, 1998
24 'Gays', Private Collection, courtesy Stephen Friedman Gallery, 2004

ART AND DELUSION

27 'The Human's Form', 2003
28 'Steal the Painting', Private Collection, 1998
29 'Movements of a Crazy Dude', Sketchbook, 1993
30/31 'Signs', Private Collection, 2004
32 'Anti-Depressants', Photograph, 2002
33 'How Much Does It Cost?', *Leotard*, BQ, Germany, 2003
34 'Pointlessness, Boredom, etc.', courtesy Galerie Yvon Lambert, France, 2004
35 'Scribble', *Enquire Within Cover*, Armpit Press, 1995
36 'Faces in the Crowd', 2001
37 'The Piece of Paper', Private Collection, 2004
38 'Picture Drawn by a Dying Man', courtesy Galerie Yvon Lambert, France, 2004
39 'Me Doing This', courtesy Stephen Friedman Gallery, 2000
40 'I Have Done My Best to Represent You', courtesy Galerie Yvon Lambert, France, 2004
41 'This Picture Has Been Caused by a Dog's Licking', Private Collection, courtesy Stephen Friedman Gallery, 2001
42 'On Monday Morning I Got Up at 8am', *Leotard*, BQ, Germany, 2003

ROUGH BEASTS

45 'The Beast Is Near', *Centre Parting*, Little Cockroach Press, 1998
46 'Elephants', Private Collection, 1999
47 'I Made This Mask', Sketchbook, 1996
48 'Dog and Coloured Background', Private Collection, 2001
49 'Pink Figure', Private Collection, 2002
50 'Bill and Ben', *Human Achievement*, Redstone Press, 2002
51 'What God Looks Like', Private Collection, 2004
52 'Light at the End of the Tunnel', Private Collection, 2004
53 'A Pirate', Private Collection, 2002
54 'In This World There Are Beasts', courtesy Galerie Yvon Lambert, France, 2004
55 'Giant Eating Man', Private Collection, 2001
56 'Artist Eaten by Wolf', courtesy Galerie Yvon Lambert, France, 2004

MEDICAL MATTERS

59 'Anatomy', courtesy Galerie Francesca Pia, Switzerland, 2004
60 'The Doctors', *Do Not Bend*, Redstone Press, 2001
61 'Wheelchair', Sketchbook, 1990
62/63 'Medical Chaos', Private Collection, 2000
64 'At the Hospital', *Leotard*, BQ, Germany, 2003
65 'Diagram of Transplant', *Why We Got The Sack from the Museum*, Redstone Press, 1998
66 'Migraine, Toothache', *Blocked Path*, Galleri Nicolai Wallner, Denmark, 2004
67 'Father & Son' courtesy Anton Kern Gallery, New York, 2005
68/69 'X-Ray', Photograph courtesy Stephen Friedman Gallery, 2002
70 'Me Next Please', courtesy Stephen Friedman Gallery, 2003

CATASTROPHES AND OTHER EVERYDAY EVENTS

73 'Family Photos (Torn and Discarded)', Sketchbook, 1995
74 'This Drawing Rejected by Kiddies Comic', Sketchbook, 1995
75 'Lady Connie + Major Smethwick-Brown', Sketchbook, 1989
76 'A Weird Thing Happened to the Other Me', Private Collection, 2004
77 'Short, Sharp Shock', Sketchbook, 1989
78 'No Speed Limit', courtesy Galerie Yvon Lambert, France, 2004
79 'Everything's Fine', Private Collection, 2001
80 'We Went on Holiday to Italy', Private Collection, 2000
81 'Hair', Sketchbook, 1995
82 'Down the Mines Morale Is Low', Private Collection, 2002

THE INTERPRETATION OF DREAMS

85 'These Pages Have No Numbers', *It Is It*, Nieves, 2004
86 'Being', *Leotard*, BQ, Germany, 2003
87 'Lots of Faces', Sketchbook, 1995
88 'Seizure at the Beauty Parlour', *Leotard*, BQ, Germany, 2003
89 'Fireworks', Private Collection, 2001
90 'Missing Since Thursday', *Blocked Path*, Galleri Nicolai Wallner, Denmark, 2004
91 'Felt-Tip Pens', Private Collection, courtesy Stephen Friedman Gallery, 2004
92 'Stick Figures', courtesy Stephen Friedman Gallery, 2004
93 'Statement: Frog', Private Collection, 2002
94 'High Tide', courtesy Galerie Yvon Lambert, France, 2002
95 'Glass Shelf', *Leotard*, BQ, Germany, 2003
96 'People Heap', *Blocked Path*, Galleri Nicolai Wallner, Denmark, 2004

MY STRUGGLE

99 'The First Page', Private Collection, 2004
100 'Never Trust', Sketchbook, 1993
101 'I Am Good', Drawing by Child, found material, collection David Shrigley, 2004
102 'Delivered to Your Door', courtesy Galerie Yvon Lambert, France, 2004
103 'It Has Always Been My Desire to Write Poetry', Private Collection, 2004
104 'Grey Wine', Private Collection, 2000
105 'From Now On', *Blocked Path*, Galleri Nicolai Wallner, Denmark, 2004
106 'My Only Failing', Private Collection, 2002
107 'The Knot', courtesy Galerie Yvon Lambert, France, 2004
108 'I Keep Knocking Things Over', courtesy Galerie Yvon Lambert, France, 2004
109 'What Time Is It?', Private Collection, 2004
110 'Fear, etc.', *Leotard*, BQ, Germany, 2003
111 'Hard Work', Private Collection, 2000

FURTHER READING

(AS IF YOU NEEDED MORE TO DO)

BIOG

BORN 1968 MACCLESFIELD

1970 FAMILY MOVED TO LEICESTER

1987/88 LEICESTER POLYTECHNIC
ART + DESIGN FOUNDATION COURSE

1988 - 91 GLASGOW SCHOOL OF ART

LIVES & WORKS IN GLASGOW

NEIL MULHOLLAND: LIFE IN LEICESTER

Last month I spent two years in Leicester, one of those tiny tarnished treasures in England where the concrete glistens like rot on a floating log. Leicester's abundance of parkland and newly pedestrianised shopping streets, I considered, were assured to make breathtaking subject matter for a budding watercolour artisan and disillusioned, melancholic, directionless motorway-café existentialist. And so, this decadent and effete town was neither of fixed livelihood nor of permanent quarters.

The Discomfort Inn was virtually desolate, but in those hot perfumed weeks in August it smelled like a fresh Ford Ka. Against a backdrop of war and poverty, I tested the reader's patience with lingering looks at fly-by-night lorry drivers and stopover suits in the hotel dining room. For my part I was drawn by an excruciatingly small elderly gentleman, carefully dressed in deer-stalker, kid leather gloves, Lee Cooper shades and Maoist jump-suit. His flashing LED belt buckle scrolled an eternity of expletives. I'm 22 and he scared the crap out of me. The phrase is Balzac's if I am not mistaken. He spent his days meditatively watching a little shop that nestled next to the Little Chef on the other side of the dual carriageway. It was a small Victorian two-story terrace building with several broken slates on the roof. Above the door I could still make out the word GROT in rather untidy sign-writing. As I noted the signs of backwoodsman disorder - observing Leicester's blasé pickled cultural excess, of a kind that remains almost totally invisible in rumour despite the recent efforts by W.G. Grace, Gary Lineker, David Gower and Peter Shilton - it struck me.

This ancient little English town has been associated with some greats, but none greater than this, the man described as 'the greatest artist ever', by his mother. An amateur of all the arts, he disdained to practice any, exploding in the face of an unsuspecting public in a holistic direction of beardlessness, idleness, hoboism, non-patriotism, and - the ultimate - Scottishness. His rogue scribbles of desire dispossessed wafted like sweet meat in the fading years of the last century. English versions of his foreign drawings remind us how little we know about him. My make-up liquefying by the fervour of the catering lamps only amplified my pitiful yearning and torturous fin de siècle façade. With typical blasé bohemian élan, he just grinned.

"There is so much rubbish sold under false pretences", he probably once intoned, "I decided to be honest about it." A primitive chick with subversive juices, he daringly won back public space from Public Hands. As southern businesses withdrew many of their offices in Scotland, he saw the tunnel at the end of the light, the best idea since asbestos. It was he who gave the soft sell to crap zines of poorly-made bus subculture loved the world over. In his name elegant cardboard shoebox architecture was demolished by local children seeking to accrue the bottles of fine Buckfast tonic wine for their dot. com launch parties. Of course, it's not in the rubbish: it's where you put the rubbish. Good Lord, please arm us this day with our daily waste.

Here was the dear pre-deceased; thirty-seven years of dedicated lip service at the end of his encyclopaedia of apologies. No fifteen minutes more of famine as the grinning interpreter of fading dreams in a fragile world of poetic failure. No heir to his experience of the mystery of transient things. It was late, late capitalism. The dual carriageway resembled a leather bowlarama trimmed with pimp cups. Pining to enter the establishment at the hottest idiot-savant roller disco in Loughborough, I imbibed a final sip of Flavia and glided into the shadows.

DONALD BARTHELME: THE BABY

The first thing the baby did wrong was to tear pages out of her books. So we made a rule that each time she tore a page out of a book she had to stay alone in her room for four hours, behind the closed door. She was tearing out about a page a day, in the beginning, and the rule worked fairly well, although the crying and screaming from behind the closed door was unnerving. We reasoned that that was the price that you had to pay, or part of the price you had to pay. But then as her grip improved she got to tearing out two pages at a time, which meant eight hours alone in her room, behind the closed door, which just doubled the annoyance for everybody. But she wouldn't quit doing it. And then as time went on we began getting days when she tore out three or four pages, which put her alone in her room for as much as sixteen hours at a stretch, interfering with normal feeding and worrying my wife. But I felt that if you made a rule you had to stick to it, had to be consistent, otherwise they get the wrong idea. She was about fourteen months old or fifteen months old at that point. Often, of course, she'd go to sleep, after an hour or so of yelling, that was a mercy. Her room was very nice, with a nice wooden rocking horse and practically a hundred dolls and stuffed animals. Lots of things to do in that room if you used your time wisely, puzzles and things. Unfortunately sometimes when we opened the door we'd find that she'd torn more pages out of more books while she was inside, and these pages had to be added to the total in fairness.

The baby's name was Born Dancin'. We gave the baby some of our wine, red, white, and blue, and spoke seriously to her. But it didn't do any good.

I must say she got real clever. You'd come up to her where she was playing on the floor, in those rare times when she was out of her room, and there'd be a book there, open beside her, and you'd inspect it and it would look perfectly all right. And then you'd look closely and you'd find a page that had one little corner torn, could easily pass for ordinary wear-and-tear, but I knew what she'd done, she'd torn off this little corner and swallowed it. So that had to count and it did. They will go to any lengths to thwart you. My wife said that maybe we were being too rigid and that the baby was losing weight. But I pointed out to her that the baby had a long life to live and had to live in a world with others, had to live in a world with many, many rules, and if you couldn't learn to play by the rules you were going to be left out in the cold with no character, shunned and ostracized by everyone. The longest we ever kept her in her room consecutively was eighty-eight hours, and that ended when my wife took the door off its hinges with a crowbar even though the baby still owed us twelve hours because she was working off twenty-five pages. I put the door back on its hinges and added a big lock, one that opened only if you put a magnetic card in a slot, and I kept the card.

But things didn't improve. The baby would come out of her room like a bat out of hell and rush to the nearest book, *Goodnight Moon* or whatever, and begin tearing pages out of it hand over fist. I mean there'd be thirty-four pages of *Goodnight Moon* on the floor in ten seconds. Plus the covers. I began to get a little worried. When I added up her indebtedness, in terms of hours, I could see that she wasn't going to get out of her room until 1992, if then. Also, she was looking pretty wan. She hadn't been to the park in weeks. We had more or less an ethical crisis on our hands.

I solved it by declaring that it was *all right* to tear pages out of books, and moreover, that it was all right to have *torn out* pages out of books in the past. That is one of the satisfying things about being a parent - you've got a lot of moves, each one good as gold. The baby and I sit happily on the floor, side by side, tearing out pages of books, and sometimes, just for fun, we go out on the street and smash a windshield together.

MICHAEL BRACEWELL: INTO THE SHADOW

Towards the end of the 1980s, it became apparent that many British towns and cities were gradually but perceptibly becoming identical. Once noticed, this phenomenon appeared to accelerate - and within a decade the process was complete.

Where once the distinguishing characteristics of a place - a corner, a main street, a square - had each enjoyed their own personality, now a fungus-like growth of dreary shop fronts, damp precincts and hot, airless cafés had all but taken over. Walls were thinner, ceilings lower, floors dirtier. The old institutional buildings, once representative of moral and social authority - churches and banks - were stripped of their fittings, filled with wide-screen televisions, and turned into vast, barn-like bars. All through the town, and through every town, the same two dozen or so brand names could be found, repeated over and over above the wide doorways.

On the edges of these identical towns and cities, chilly crepuscular hinterlands of carpet showrooms, DIY superstores and sportswear clearance warehouses stretched off in all directions, as far as the eye could see. And even further - because at some point on the horizon their prairie-like expanses merged with those of the adjoining conurbations, like the land masses on maps of the prehistoric world. A few fields of wiry grass, colourless in the pinkish gleam of immensely tall streetlights, were the only slight variations - a tiny swell in the sea of sameness - that occurred within the landscape.

To entertain the inhabitants of this new mono-environment, the various strands of the national media came up with cheap, nasty, tasteless gimmicks. In addition to which, strong alcohol was made available in the same flavours as children's sweets and snacks. Toffee Crisp flavoured vodka shots, Bubblegum tequila, Monster Munch Bacardi. The latest cars were named after the most popular dishes on Indian take-away menus: The Vauxhall Korma; the new Fiat Madras. Mobile phones destroyed the distinction between public and personal space.

Young women started to talk like camp gay men. When you applied for a mortgage, you were given a voucher for a free Mochaccino Latte. The middle two shelves of magazines in every newsagents shop comprised a broad horizontal stripe, reddish orange in colour, of identical looking young women, every one of whom had been photographed with her thumbs in the waistband of her knickers. Gratuitous male aggression was not only encouraged, but celebrated. Local newspapers became directories of horror. Every week, it seemed, unbelievably vile and stupid people did unbelievably vile and stupid things to each other, and to anyone or anything which happened to cross their path. Animals, in particular, suffered at their hands. Kittens were shot in the face at close range; ducklings were taken from a pond and stamped on; a dog was hung from a tree in a sack and beaten to death.

The wealthiest and most fashionable people in this new Britain were made even wealthier and more fashionable, by poorer people who paid to look at pictures of them going to private parties and expensive restaurants, or to read accounts of their luxurious lifestyles and love affairs. Pensioners began to dress like rappers. Clumsy fist fights broke out between businessmen on crowded trains. Toddlers were known to stab one another with screwdrivers. Truancy was rife. Most jobs were dull and poorly paid. The weather became first mild, then humid. The sun looked bigger, and redder, and lower in the sky. Dead polar bears were found washed up on the shores of Scandinavia.

These events did not occur in a way that was particularly dramatic, let alone apocalyptic. Rather, they had an atherosclerotic, sluggish momentum - their progress was incremental, as opposed to declamatory. It was as though history had ended, and the concept of a future, too; and all that was left was the sweeping up, at the close of a hot, windy day of low white skies. Horses, their ribs showing through their skin, stood very still on the edges of toxic landfill sites. Jut-jawed, heavy-browed, tattooed on calf or small of back, territorially hostile, the last of the consumers became more like scavengers. Their expressions were hostile, and they were swift to take offence. Their children were first spoilt, then cursed for being alive.

It was only when one managed to somehow gain a great height over this new landscape, and look down upon it, that you realised what had happened. In the space of a relatively short amount of time, the whole of Britain had turned into one enormous shop. And everything that had not assisted the shop in making more profit, had been either forced into dereliction or declared eccentric. And thus, after just a few years, all that was lovely, or gentle, or, to use an old-fashioned word, 'seemly' - had been destroyed.

———————————

David Shrigley is an artist who sees the world in terms of its moral X-ray, so to speak. The son of Christian fundamentalists, his formative years included an exposure to a purely Biblical interpretation of the world. Despite rejecting the tenets of this outlook as he grew older, its imprint can still be seen, in a refined and refracted version of itself, across the landscape and vision of his art. There is a sense in which this moral view, minutely balanced between absurdist satire and genuine unease (fear, paranoia and anxiety) is expressed in Shrigley's art through the rhetoric of outsiderdom.

Stick men with evil grinning faces, obsessively cross-hatched maps and diagrams, forlorn memos concerning some tragic or horrific event: the world described by Shrigley's art is that of a perpetually darkened quotidian; a world in which, as his drawing 'Result' describes, Evil eventually beats Good by 5-4 on penalties, after extra time. This art seems to reach us as urgent reports from a sufferer of delusional episodes, or as official dictates from a curdled authority; or like the rantings of a misanthropic loner. In '*Blanket of Filth*' (Armpit Press, 1994), the first drawing - a touchingly incompetent self-portrait - proclaims, "I stand alone because my words are unacceptable to others".

The old Hollywood musical adage that "You can study Shakespeare and have nothing to eat/Slip on a banana skin, the world's at your feet" is particularly true of Shrigley. Go to any art gallery or arts institution bookshop in the world, and the one artist bound to be reproonted in the stock is Shrigley. His art has become a form of postmodern esperanto, its humour doing the work of theory, aesthetics, conceptualism or dogma.

FRANZ KAFKA

THE CARES OF A FAMILY MAN

Some say the word Odradek is of Slavonic origin, and try to account for it on that basis. Others again believe it to be of German origin, only influenced by Slavonic. The uncertainty of both interpretations allows one to assume with justice that neither is accurate, especially as neither of them provides an intelligent meaning of the word.

No one, of course, would occupy himself with such studies if there were not a creature called Odradek. At first glance it looks like a flat star-shaped spool of thread, and indeed it does seem to have thread wound upon it; to be sure, they are only old, broken-off bits of thread knotted and tangled together, of the most varied sorts and colors. But it is not only a spool, for a small wooden crossbar sticks out of the middle of the star, and another small rod is joined to that at a right angle. By means of this latter rod on one side and one of the points of the star on the other, the whole thing can stand upright as if it has two legs.

One is tempted to believe that the creature once had some sort of intelligible shape and is now only a broken-down remnant. Yet this does not seem to be the case; at least there is no sign of it; nowhere is there an unfurnished or unbroken surface to suggest anything of the kind; the whole thing looks senseless enough but in its own way perfectly finished. In any case, closer scrutiny is impossible, since Odradek is extraordinarily nimble and can never be laid hold of.

He lurks by turns in the garret, the stairway, the lobbies, the entrance hall. Often for months on end he is not to be seen; then he has presumably moved into other houses; but he always comes faithfully back to our house again. Many a time when you go out of the door and he happens just to be leaning directly beneath you against the banisters you feel inclined to speak to him. Of course, you put no difficult questions to him, you treat him - he is diminutive that you cannot help it - rather like a child, "Well, what's your name?" you ask him. "Odradek," he says. "And where do you live?" "No fixed abode," he says and laughs; but it is only the kind of laughter that has no lungs behind it. It sounds rather like the rustling of fallen leaves. And that is usually the end of the conversation. Even these answers are not always forthcoming; often he stays mute for a long time, as wooden as his appearance.

I ask myself, to no purpose, what is likely to happen to him? Can he possibly die? Anything that dies has had some kind of aim in life, some kind of activity, which has worn out; but that does not apply to Odradek. Am I to suppose, then, that he will always be rolling down the stairs, with ends of thread trailing after him, right before the feet of my children, and my children's children? He does no harm to anyone that can see; but the idea that he is likely to survive me I find almost painful.

AT NIGHT

Deeply lost in the night. Just as one sometimes lowers one's head to reflect, thus to be utterly lost in the night. All around people are asleep. It's just play acting, an innocent self-deception, that they sleep in houses, in safe beds, under blankets; in reality they have flocked together as they had once upon a time and again later in a deserted region, a camp in the open, a countless number of men, an army, a people, under a cold sky on cold earth, collapsed where once they stood, forehead pressed on the arm, face to the ground, breathing quietly. And you are watching, are one of the watchmen, you find the next one by brandishing a burning stick from the brushwood pile beside you. Why are you watching? Someone must watch, it is said. Someone must be there.

RESOLUTIONS

To lift yourself out of a miserable mood, even if you have to do it by strength of will, should be easy. I force myself out of my chair, stride around the table, exercise my head and neck, make my eyes sparkle, tighten the muscles around them. Defy my own feelings, welcome A. enthusiastically supposing he comes to see me, amiably tolerate B, in my room, swallow all that is said at C's, whatever pain and trouble it may cost me, in long draughts.

Yet even if I manage that, one single slip, and a slip cannot be avoided, will stop the whole process, easy and painful alike, and I will have to shrink back into my own circle again.

So perhaps the best resource is to meet everything passively, to make yourself an inert mass, and, if you feel that you are being carried away, not to let yourself be lured into taking a single unnecessary step, to stare at others with the eyes of an animal, to feel no compunction, in short, with your own hand to throttle down whatever ghostly life remains in you, that is, to enlarge the final peace of the graveyard and let nothing survive save that.

A characteristic movement in such a condition is to run your little finger along your eyebrows.

FELLOWSHIP

We are five friends, one day we came out of a house one after the other, first one came and placed himself beside the gate, then the second came, or rather he glided through the gate like a little ball of quicksilver, and placed himself near the first one, then came the third, then the fourth, then the fifth. Finally we all stood in a row. People began to notice us, they pointed at us and said: Those five just came out of that house. Since then we have been living together; it would be a peaceful life if it weren't for a sixth continually trying to interfere. He doesn't do us any harm, but he annoys us, and that is harm enough; why does he intrude where he is not wanted? We don't know him and don't want him to join us. There was a time, of course, when the five of us did not know one another, either; and it could be said that we still don't know one another, but what is possible and can be tolerated by the five of us is not possible and cannot be tolerated with this sixth one. In any case, we are five and don't want to be six. And what is the point of this continual being together anyhow? It is also pointless for the five of us, but here we are together and will remain together; a new combination, however, we do not want, just because of our experiences. But how is one to make all this clear to the sixth one? Long explanations would almost amount to accepting him in our circle, so we prefer not to explain and not to accept him. No matter how he pouts his lips we push him away with our elbows, but however much we push him away, back he comes.

MEL GOODING: THE LAST WORD

O the great God of Theory, he's just a pencil stub, a chewed stub with a worn eraser at the end of a huge scribble. (Charles Simic)

Bringing Shrigley to book is not easy. He owns up to inducing anxiety. But, then, it's not his anxiety that we feel as we turn the pages: it's ours. It is there, waiting to haunt us, before he confirms our worst nightmares. Shrigley makes visible the darkness we all inhabit.

'Better a dreadful doubt confronted, a fear outfaced, a weakness acknowledged' the therapists might say. But Shrigley's not your therapist! He's not there to help you.

'But', we might be tempted to think, 'he confirms that we are not alone; we're all in it together!' That's the point of it all: Solidarity! But no. Shrigley isn't there to raise your spirits. Like every great satirist he's a stern moralist. He shows us where we are and how it is. How you feel about that is your problem, not his. He offers naught for your comfort.

There's no great God of Theory behind this contingent universe: there's no theory of everything, or of anything, that is remotely helpful when you're touching the void. This is not a book of explanations or of consolations. It's a book of revelations. Apocalypse now! Only this time we can laugh. Sometimes, laughing at Shrigley, I feel that's the only thing we can do.

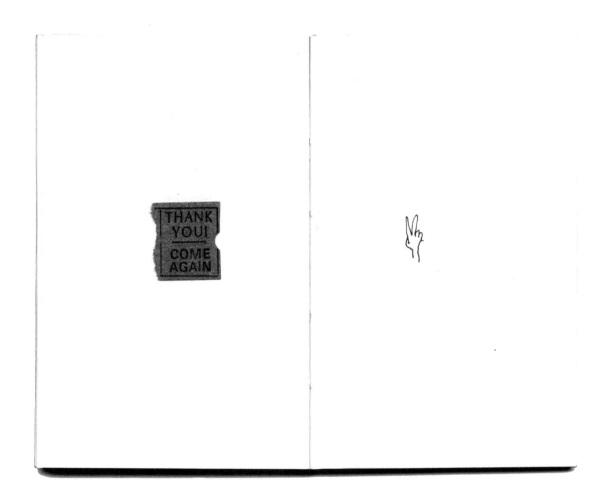